THE HEART
—— Is Not ——
ENOUGH

Habits of Educators Who **Care** for Modern Kids

SHIRLEY PREYAN

Email: info@shirleypreyan.com

Editing and Interior Formatting
House Capacity Publishing LLC
www.HouseCapacity.com

Cover Designer: Ajibola Creative Artz

ISBN-13: 979-8-218-06670-3

For the kids who cared for me, as I learned to care for them.
For Wayne, who cared for me as I cared for the kids.
For Everly, who cares for me.

A NOTE TO READERS

Names of students have been changed to protect the
identities and confidentiality of all parties involved.

Contents

PREFACE

I have failed so many kids. Each time that I wanted deeply in my heart to "save" a child or move the needle forward for them, I found myself asking why it wasn't working when I was giving so much effort. As I honed my skills and gained experience as an educator and disciplinarian of kids, I wished for a magic wand to go back and have a do-over with so many of the kids I worked with in the earlier stages of my career. I knew, in my young, developing opinion, what those kids needed; I just didn't know how to give it to them.

I felt a lot of frustration working through challenging scenarios with students because I cared so deeply. Care was supposed to be the key ingredient. There were barriers that I wanted them to overcome, but I was also underdeveloped in my experience working with kids. I was certain that I liked kids, and they seemed to like me, too. Actually, I realized that I *really* cared about children. I shared their backgrounds, and I cared about what they were experiencing. I knew I was in the right place as an educator, I just didn't know how to deliver the care they so desperately needed. That left me feeling quite discontented early in my education career.

As a school administrator, I've worked with many students in a one-on-one environment in my office or in the hallway. I've worked with hundreds of students at a time in cafeterias and auditoriums. I've worked with kids who didn't immediately understand my disposition, didn't care for me, adored me, and everything in between. I pride myself on being able to create meaningful connections with all kids, despite their challenges. As I would work with students, I started to understand that being one person who can work with all kids has very little value in the larger context of a school.

All adults in a school building should be able to deliver the same level of care to kids. Relying on a few individuals to govern the most challenging students creates a disciplinary handicap for the campus. As society developed and more kids began to operate outside of what we saw as normal, it seemed that the gap between the educators who understood how to work with modern kids and those who didn't was widening.

I couldn't seem to pinpoint the disconnect that occurred when I worked to de-escalate a student in the hallway and what happened when they returned to class. I didn't understand why kids would listen to a few educators in the school building but not others. Even if students "listened" there was often still a repetitive cycle of chasing calm until the behavior showed up again. The conversation among teachers was growing increasingly negative and my own love for education was starting to become tainted. That's why I'm writing this book.

I am an 11-year career educator who has served over 2000 students. As a teacher, I've taught reading, math, and social studies in the middle school grades. I've taught classes of 60+ kids at once when the teacher across the hall was promoted and there was no one to teach the students. I've scored over 90% passing on state exams and won national teaching awards. I've coached cheerleading and volleyball. In leadership roles, I've served as a lead teacher, department head, reading and math instructional coach, assistant principal, and school co-founder.

I've worked on a wide variance of campuses that included the school where parents send their students to the "good side of the town" for a better education, next door to a housing project, in a mixed-income, choice, progressive school, and in a GED center where I had no certification but became an instructor. I have worked as a teacher, instructional coach, and assistant principal in an Improvement Ready 5 turnaround school that was listed as the worst in the state. I've had an opportunity to build a school of choice after working on a team to create a vision for the kind of school I believed was missing in education, which included writing a lengthy proposal and going before powerful district committees. I've worked on writing grants that received over $850,000 for schools, and, of course, done my share of Donors Choose projects for my class library.

I've stood in line to buy hundreds of composition notebooks for kids, driven kids home from cheer practice, and walked them home in the rain. I've organized and taken entire schools and grade levels on field trips. And I'm incredibly proud that I've taken 14 kids, seven of whom lived in a housing project, to Italy to present at a global conference. I've been the first one in the building and the last. Sometimes, on the same day. I've broken up my share of fights, had my share of parent complaints, and my share of teacher complaints. I've been to lots of education conferences and toured the best and worst schools from California to New York, and I'm committed to being a lifelong educator.

My "why" links back to all of the teachers at Vandenberg Elementary School who cared for me: Ms. Gamble, Ms. Cole, Ms. Woodall, Ms. Steele, Ms. Swayne, Mr. Shulam, Ms. Ryan, Ms. Samuel, Ms. Giles, Mr. Sanders, Mr. Davis, Ms. Dixon, Mr. Claiborne, and my elementary school principal, Shirley Daggs-Monroe, (I recall their names from memory). My "why" links back to Coffey Middle School and Cass Technical Highschool where Ms. Heading, Ms. Haldane, Ms. Bickerstaff, Ms. Snead, Ms. Willis, Ms. Chillis, Mr. Jones, Dean Sanders, Mr. El-Amin, Gloria Nixon, and the Inside Out Literary Poetry Program cared for me. My "why" links back to my grandmother who took in six of her grandchildren at 72 years old from the foster care system. Most importantly, my "why" lies in my first classroom, room 305, which led me to a cemetery in Bastrop, Louisiana.

It can not explain to you the pain that comes from burying a student. It is something that I hope you never have to experience in your professional career. Most especially, your unequivocal, favorite student. Without question, I wanted to help Robert. He shared my brother Robert's name and reminded me of my brother, Anthony, who was killed by a police officer at age sixteen in 2002. Robert was smart, charismatic, helpful, and was protective of others when he noticed they were being mistreated. Everyone knew him as Tanka.

"Ms. Bolden, if everybody is supposed to be a leader, then who is going to be following them? .... "Ms. Bolden, Jay-Z is old, his music ain't hittin' like that." I can hear his voice still. I hear others, too.

"That boy is going to end up dead or in jail."

"Some kids just aren't going to make it."

I still have the speaking notes on my phone from his funeral. Something won't let me delete them.

I wore the pair of pants that he deemed "teacher pants" as I spoke at his funeral:

"We suspend brilliant black boys and promote brilliant Asian boys. We send brilliant black boys to alternative schools and give brilliant white boys slaps on the wrist."

I can still hear the sound of sadness in that warm church sanctuary. I remember looking at him in his casket. I wondered if he still heard those teachers' voices, "...dead or in jail." I remember taking him to Macy's to get an outfit for his sixteenth birthday because I had planned a meeting with a mentor for him. I remember the moment I realized he was turning fifteen in the sixth grade but he passed every test I gave him without even trying. I remember working with him to be moved forward to the 8th grade so he would have a chance. I remember many things, and I hold those memories dear. He should still be here.

Education is a strange field. You pour knowledge along with your heart and soul into students for nine months at a time. Then those students move on and you do it again. As a school administrator, you watch students grow up from being nervously dropped off by a parent to confidently buying Valentine's Day presents for their eighth-grade girlfriends. You hope that you have done enough for those kids or at least held the line steady in their life. Most of us are well-meaning educators who are doing and giving our absolute best, and I can sense that we're hurting as a profession.

Beyond my work in the classroom, I care for boys and girls because someone cared for me. As a child, I was given a life that required resilience. I was born to parents who were navigating a drug addiction with nine children, placed into foster care to be adopted by my loving Grandmother, unfortunately navigating sexual abuse, and placed back into foster care into adulthood after unsuccessful adoptions. Despite my tumultuous upbringing, many people along the way cared for me, and something in me was unwilling to not return the gesture. I am grateful for every human, church member, after-school program, well-meaning adult, and stranger who cared enough to plant, water, or cultivate seeds that grew within me. I must pay that forward.

When I think back to my first K-12 classroom in room 305, I am pushed back even further to recall the GED center I worked in prior to education. I was fresh out of college with a journalism and women's studies degree from Michigan State University. The journalism field was navigating the onset of the digital media takeover, and so on a whim, I applied to Teach for America. I was waitlisted for a year and needed a job. I was a freelance and magazine intern and needed a more steady income.

I eventually accepted a well-paying job through a connection to our local community college's vice-provost. This was also the onset of digital education learning programs. In the GED program, the students were to log into the computer and follow the tutorials to prepare them for their GED test. I particularly remember one student, Mr. Joe, who was over 60 years old. His first question was, "How do I turn on a computer?"

The students were not only incapable of learning from the poorly programmed computer simulations, but they were also struggling with the consumable textbooks, too. My job was to sit at the front desk and allow them to sign in and out. I was to assist with minor technical issues that arose, but things didn't go that way. Somehow, I had managed to find myself at a table with students, eventually standing and delivering lessons with no idea what I was doing. Eventually, the college allowed me to be a teacher though I had no certification. I cared for those men and women and they embraced me. When I entered the classroom as a sixth-grade reading teacher the next school year, I could see even more clearly that at some point someone didn't know how to care for those adults when they were boys and girls.

As I matriculated into school leadership, I read all of the important books. There are many well-written, profound research books about school discipline that describe the causes of behavior challenges you see in students in today's urban schools. I read so thoroughly about the problems that exist in education. I read about administrative responsibility and the key ingredients of success to ensure students would academically perform. I read about the conspiracies to destroy public education and the need to revolutionize schools into social-emotional technologically advanced cooperative learning workshop spaces.

Though we were using all of the textbook protocols, everyone in my school building was sharing how exhausted they were from the complexities of navigating education pre and post covid. Somehow the solutions offered by newly emerging valuable practices seemed to be missing something about the everyday physiological challenges that were beneath the surface. There are many anecdotal articles written about the great resignation and migration of amazing educators into various career paths outside of the school building. Even my Facebook timeline is riddled with posts of frustrated teachers trying to recover from tough days.

We can discuss and debate the problem to no end, but because I care for boys and girls, I am unwilling to keep talking about it. This is not a book about the problems with kids, administrators, public education, modern-day parenting, or returning to the good ol' days when kids listened to their elders. This is a book about the habits of educators who care for modern children. I'm not a parenting expert or a policy expert. But I sure do love kids, teachers, school leaders, and parents alike.

This book is for everyone who desperately finds themselves wanting to do their best caring for kids but just can't seem to figure out why it's not working the way you intend. It's for every absent educator who is frustrated with their own burnout but knows for certain that they hope to end up back in education when they've replenished their heart. It's for the teacher who has lost their spark and the teacher who's developing their spark alike. It's for the aspiring administrator who wants to get school discipline right. The administrator who has lost their touch and can't understand the teacher's frustrations in the classroom anymore. It's for the superintendent looking to get back in touch. It is for anyone who understands that if we don't care for boys and girls we shouldn't be near a school building, children's church, summer camp, after-school program, or mental health service for kids. Simply put, it's for people who care for kids.

So many of us well-meaning educators can see that we're giving our best, but for some reason, it's not received in the ways we intend. We understand how to manage a classroom but still get lost in a few of the difficult nuanced moments and we want help working through them. We can see the trust between schools and parents dissipating. We observe the contentious relationships between teachers and administrators, and for the sake of the children, we all want to get this right.

This book is filled with personal stories from my career in education. Nearly all of these stories are embarrassing, but I tell them with pride because, as a former journalist, I know the power of a personal story. I never got it all the way right, but I always wanted to and I will keep trying. I have worked with so many amazing educators over the years; every single one of them gave their best most of the time. In education training, we miss the moment to train teachers about the reality of when the heart clashes with their skill set. If we're not trained on the proactive options, reactive options become the solution. We're humans, we're not robots. The relational discipline skills that we have as teachers are not an automatic upgrade that occurs every so many years. We're all learning. Besides, no one gave us a heads-up that the children were changing.

This book is not about putting the children in their place, it's about showing them how to operate in the world as they are and supporting them in change and growth as needed. I am revisiting my original statement: I have failed so many kids. I wish that I could have a do-over with the opportunity to incorporate some of these skills that I have learned along the way. My hope is that these habits will be instilled in every human and well-meaning adult who encounters kids. I acknowledge the complexity of this work and hope that this book reduces the number of students left behind and uncared for.

Part I

WHY ISN'T THE HEART ENOUGH?

As a first-year teacher, I had an eighth-period class that educators affectionately referred to as their "terror block." It was a double-blocked 90-minute reading language arts course of students I absolutely adored. They affirmed the reason I pursued the education profession. They had reading and behavioral challenges, special needs, and language barriers. At twenty-three years old, I knew that I loved them and that I was going to change their lives. When I met those students, I could feel the emergence and innocence of the savior complex sprouting within me, coupled with my pure intentions.

They were a group of witty, clever kids who found humor in small things. About six of those students had failed the year prior. They were assigned to my reading class because they were students of the other reading teachers during the previous school year. They were having their second turn at-bat with the sixth grade. This was a group of boys who desperately needed academic intervention beyond what I understood and was able to give them as a first-year teacher.

Even though I was inexperienced, I was determined to help them—my heart *needed* to help them.

I would struggle to manage this particular class and would sometimes dread the end of the day with them. One day, I went to school Spongebob-ready. My best lesson was prepared, and I was adorned in a black pencil skirt and black blazer. Facebook memories reminded me of my mindset. My status that morning before school was, "The devil created terror blocks, but God created seating charts." As soon as they began shuffling into the room, I set the tone that I was not going to put up with any foolishness. Harold chuckled as I attempted to look them sternly in the eyes. Everyone was buying it but Harold.

"You're trying to act different today, Ms. Bolden."

I gave everyone new seats. I attempted to separate the boys in a north, south, east, west pattern. I even rearranged the seats during my planning period specifically for this class. I believed that if I faced them towards the back of the classroom, I could eliminate some of the hallway visibility that caused them to keep asking to take what became extended bathroom breaks and clustering outside my door in the halls. I broke the wheel on my SMART Board as I dragged it to the back of the room. I rehearsed my lesson as I tracked around the class, clicking through the slides of my

PowerPoint and placing pencils on desks. I inhaled using deep breaths and tried to practice what we now refer to as mindfulness. I stationed myself at the door ready to view the hall and the students as they began their "Do-now." I was at my best; I could feel it.

About forty-five minutes into class, my performance was wearing off and they were beginning to chatter. Admittedly, those little voices behind my back as I tried to read "All Summer in a Day" triggered me. They always did. I couldn't figure out why I couldn't get these eleven to thirteen-year-olds to listen to me. It felt like disrespect. Besides, I was wearing kitten heels and a black blazer. Harold made his signature "ha-ha" noise and that was all I could take. I lost my cool and professional tact.

I ran to the door and screamed out as loudly as I could without the other teachers hearing, "Y'all getting on my got damn nerves."

Warm tears ran down my face as I attempted to slam the door as a show of my frustration. The door didn't slam. It was on a stopper that forced the door into a slow graze towards the threshold. Harold yelled out, "ha ha!" again, mimicking the voice that Nelson used on "The Simpsons." This laugh was his thing, and the other kids fed into it each time. It was his favorite way to derail class.

Embarrassed, crushed, and defeated, I sat down on the floor in the hallway outside my classroom and sobbed in heartfelt frustration. Those were the typical tears of a determined, first-year teacher who was really, really trying. Ms. Binfield, the near-retirement teacher across the hall, saw the whole exchange. She took me to get ice cream after school. I sat in Paciugo Gelato wearing a black business suit and kitten heels eating cookies and cream ice cream on the day that I was supposed to conquer my 8th-period class. I felt small, like I was 10 years old.

***

My first year as an administrator, I cared deeply for Marisol. She was one of a kind. Marisol came from a close-knit Hispanic family that was navigating their way through a large household and a father who had recently passed from a terminal illness. Her father was the heart of their patriarchal family. He spoiled each of his daughters in preparation for his transition. Marisol was family-oriented, giving, sassy, privileged, emotionally challenged, grieving, and frankly, insubordinate. When she would hear me coming, she'd scream, yell, run into classrooms, and play a hide-and-seek game for about sixty seconds before willingly coming to my office. Once in my office, she would share intimate details of her struggles and family life. I'd push her to complete a breathing exercise, go to her home to get her set up for counseling services, and do many other things to support her and her family. My efforts didn't seem to be making any difference.

If Marisol was in your class, there was no learning taking place. Marisol would distract every student. She would chase kids around the room, talk back to the teacher, leave the classroom, and rile up the class. I didn't know how to work with her beyond my office. All of the phone-calls home to mom weren't helping. I felt quite vulnerable and exposed as teachers watched me struggle to manage her in the hallways, especially because in my office there was a different tone. I was supposed to be different and having a positive relationship was supposed to work. What was I missing?

With eleven years in education, I have plenty of these stories, and I am sure you do, too. I share them to highlight one thing: I have a heart for kids. I very much want to tell you that having a heart for kids is what it takes to be able to work through challenging moments with students. You can love kids so much that through the combined power of telekinesis and osmosis a student will automatically receive all of your love and care. In the words of my grandmother, "They will straighten up and fly right." Unfortunately, the heart is not enough. Caring for kids is not singularly a matter of the heart or mindset. Responsibly caring for kids in a school or extracurricular setting requires tangible skills. I believe that all educators can have deep meaningful relationships with kids if they knew how to care for children. And today's modern children bring in new dynamics that we didn't anticipate. Simply put, the heart is not enough because old habits don't work with new kids.

We're Overstimulated and Emotionally Depleted

Our hearts for kids are so big and the work is so new and challenging that it's contributing to our emotional burnout. Beyond caring, we need modernized skills to work with today's modern students. There was a time in my own career when raising your voice with students was enough. It expressed that you were serious and students would stop engaging in unfavorable behaviors. Yelling is becoming less and less effective, and it should have never been practiced in schools. It is rooted in old hierarchies that suggest that students "do what you're told." I have vivid memories of Matilda's principal admonishing her with Roald Dahl's words, "I'm smart, you're dumb. I'm big, you're little. I'm right, you're wrong, and there's nothing you can do about it." In those days, we sought to control students as a form of showing respect, and it wasn't always healthy.

We must admit that our relationship with modern-day children is complicated and emotionally taxing. As children, many of us were "put in our place." As adults, we carry deep dismay for those harmful old-school practices that we still replay in our minds. Even so, we face a new reality today: some kids and parents don't seem to respond to teachers with the same respect that we did. We even find ourselves feeling a sense of guilt, remembering how harsh words and tough love made us feel damaged and less than. We Gen Z, Millennials, and Gen Xers find ourselves seeking healing from the unintentional wounds from the adults of our childhood and seeking to avoid planting the same seeds of negativity in our children.

The emotional burden of caring for kids today is exasperated by the fact that we are a more emotional society. Since we are a more emotional society, it's painful to work with such a big heart and still receive such opposition from various sources. This is eroding our love for education.

Children today are born into the days of personalization, choice and voice as parental rearing has evolved over the years. Second chances are a norm, as are third and fourth chances. It's okay to admit that we need to fine-tune our approaches as this doesn't always align with our upbringing and it has an uncomfortable fit into the context of education as we've known it. How am I supposed to give grace and hold high expectations? Similarly, as modern educators, we see the value in using counseling as opposed to punitive practices. We understand that restorative discipline is necessary but still feel the very human blow to our ego when kids return from the principal's office smiling with a green lollipop. It's so far from everything we have known. That can feel contradictory.

For me, toys were not allowed at schools. Today, fidget spinners, sand gardens, stress balls, and gadgets are a healthy outlet for kids, and confiscating a child's items is highly frowned upon. I once took up a toy chicken that made a loud squawking noise from a student. Somehow, I lost the chicken and had to buy a new one for the student after a lengthy conversation with a parent. I googled "loud chicken" and surely there it was in all of its annoying glory. Kids today are receiving the necessary grace that should have been afforded to all children. Grace and parental advocacy are no longer for children of influence; it's for everyone. That's a good thing—a good, uncomfortable thing.

As a young child, I was required to address adults as "ma'am" or "sir." I was required to use their full names, not just "Ms." If I ever referred to a "Mrs." as a "Ms." I received an ear full. Every adult had the right to correct and discipline me, and I was required to listen because they were an adult.

In education, we have blamed many people for how kids interact with adults today.

"It's bad parenting."

"These kids need therapy."

"There aren't enough consequences anymore."

"Babies are having babies."

"Everybody wants to be these kids' friends."

"We took prayer out of school."

"We took the paddle out of school."

"We took extra-curricular activities out of school."

None of these things are singularly the problem. We have reasonably and expectedly progressed into a more emotionally intelligent society that is disassociating from hierarchies built on distributing power to some and not to others. That redistribution of power to students' voices and choices is contributing to the emotional burnout that we feel. We are trying to meet all kids at their emotional levels without being able to rely on the consequences that we used to know like phone calls home, suspension, detention, and more transparently, yelling and belittling. That is new for most of us.

As an entire society, we are allowed to express our emotions in ways that we have never been able to. The days of colonization have been replaced with diplomacy. We promote peace and conversation, even in our relationship with children. Even many of our relationships with our supervisors at work are less directive and are more collaborative. Old wisdom on classroom management meant "Don't smile 'til Christmas." Kids were to never know anything about you as a human. You were never required to "like" your teachers.

If there was a teacher you didn't like, your parents likely explained to you that your teacher's job was to teach you, not to be your friend. There was a time when we accepted social hierarchies as they were. As we dismantle all of the systems of the world that promote any forms of supremacy, the power dynamics that exist between kids and teachers and schools and parents are one of them.

***

Today, parents are no longer as trusting of others to discipline their children as they were in previous generations. Take my older brother, Robert, for example. Robert has always been a bit of a rocker. When he sat down, he naturally rocked forward and backward when he was excited, nervous, or bored. Once, his teacher tied him to a seat with a jump rope to get him to stop rocking because it was an annoyance to her. Now, I was a second grader when this happened to my brother, who was a third grader, so I have no idea what happened behind closed doors. But in 2022, there would have been a viral, widespread video and tons of commentary and controversy about this event. Some teachers would have argued that teachers are human and have a breaking point. Lots of viewers on the internet would have diagnosed him with ADHD. Many parents would have been outraged at the way kids are being treated by teachers. That wasn't the case in 1992.

Working with kids in the days of yesteryear came with an expectation of having rigid firmness with moments of softness and understanding. Today, working with kids is much more emotionally complex as we are taught to lead with openness. As a child, I hated the idea of a parent ever being called; today, some kids welcome it. At times, students text their parents when they get a bad grade, and the parent schedules a meeting to demand that it be changed. Some kids know that their parents will advocate for them whether they are right or wrong. For many of us, this is new. Does this parent not respect my judgment as a professional? I am certain that our parents advocated for us when we were younger. I am certain that my strong-willed grandmother met with our school principal; we just weren't in the room when it happened. Times have changed.

One of the starkest differences between the teacher who tied my brother to the seat and teachers today was that she had a long-standing relationship with the community.

This was true of nearly all the teachers at our elementary school. My siblings, twenty years my senior, and I had the same teachers. Back then, those teachers were younger with their maiden names, but they were the same teachers working in the same school. Today, this is much rarer. Teachers and families are more mobile and trust doesn't run as deep because we don't share the same history with school staff. Parents don't have the same level of trust that the principal they've known forever and was likely their teacher or older children's teacher will handle the situation in a way that they trust. Today, we speak to all systems of power, including the power systems that exist in schools.

Most of us are overstimulated. Inflation is affecting the already meager pay that teachers receive. Political conversations about everything from critical race theory to when kids should be exposed to gay pride flags are hijacking discussions on education. We're considering referring to slavery as voluntary relocation. The even more daunting reality of school shootings is making it dangerous for us to even want to be inside of a school. How are we supposed to focus with all of this going on? Many well-intentioned parents are seeking to protect what their kids are exposed to and are doing their best to maintain their trust in schools. It's all so confusing. And somehow, we're still supposed to keep teaching long vowels. We love this work so much that though we are losing hope, we keep showing up, and it emotionally depletes us.

When we encounter a difficult moment with a student it feels like a sensory, emotional overload. I am navigating all of these other things in the world and this student not having a pencil is pushing me to a breaking point. We all know, it's not about the pencil; it is about everything else that we are feeling. This student just cursed at me and they are back in my room fifteen minutes later, and I'm just supposed to keep teaching proportions. It seems that this parent is validating this student's behavior; let me continue my lesson on theme. I've worked all night on this master schedule and a parent is asking which idiot worked on the schedule and is berating me because there are no more seats in the Latin class.

Today, we are lauded for being understanding and empathetic and seeking to find the root cause of many of our own behaviors as adults. We talk more openly about therapy and mental health services than ever before. It's even more telling that we talk about these things in direct relation to kids. We're seeking to remove many of the issues we face as adults by doing a better job taking care of kids. The wisdom we have gleaned from our lived experiences has made the connection between our current challenges and how we were raised as children.

What Exactly Is a Modern Kid?

As we go forward, I need to stop and define what I mean when I say "modern kids." First, let me note that the children of today didn't ask to be modern. This is simply their reality. They're not going to shine shoes for a nickel so they can buy a newspaper to read the new Peanuts cartoon. Most importantly, they're not better or worse than kids from previous generations, and regardless of the uncomfortable nature of their generational progression, all kids are deserving of care.

Many of the attributes of today's kids are byproducts of the woes of our childhoods, and so we socialize our children differently. As we socialize our children differently, they are different. I know, *shocker*. As an entire society, we are seeking liberation. We just weren't quite prepared to feel the discomfort of liberated children. Children are always a reflection of the adults who have taught them how to navigate the world we created for them.

It's also true that we don't always immediately recognize our own reflection. What I mean here is that we've created the space for us to thrive as adults with all the grace that we need but hope to instill accountability in the children in the ways that our elders instilled things in us, through fear tactics. We've created space for conversation and cooperation with children but still, at times, want the kids to respond to commands immediately. It's contradictory that we still want to borrow a little from the past that these children have never known to control them. Can you see the gap here? Kids don't need to pay the dues from our past.

I say this gently, but when we're really trying our best to use all of the new gentle practices, it makes us feel like we're losing some of our power. Your power is not related to dominion over children. We can admit that there is an uncomfortableness in deconstructing old habits to provide children with some of the kindness we craved as children. We acknowledge that generations before us were operating with the resources that they had. With all of the stringent rules that we had growing up, we still did all the same things that kids of this generation did. We just did it in private, hiding from the adults to avoid being shamed.

When I refer to modern students, I'm thinking of the attributes that set them apart from previous generations. In the basic form, kids will always be kids. Of course, there will be some beautiful things like the exploration of self, missing teeth, giggles, growth spurts, first heartbreaks, the first time driving, and many other firsts. On the other hand, there will always be some snotty noses, exploring what it means to lie, some stealing of cookies, and some sneaking out of the house.

To appropriately sum up the definition of "modern kids," I like to use this acronym:

> **C:** Choice-Driven
>
> **A:** Access-Driven
>
> **R:** Relationally-Driven
>
> **E:** Emotionally Expressive

Choice-Driven

We know that today, kids are born into choice. When today's students were toddlers, they opened an iPad and decided to play their game of choice. In doing so, they likely selected an avatar and dressed it in whatever outfit felt most appealing to them. They added a picture that brought them joy to the lock screen and homepage and, likely, updated the photo as their interest changed throughout the years.

Maybe every kid didn't have an iPad, but more than likely there was a smartphone or some sort of device nearby that gave them lots of options. I'm not referring to the sort of preferences that led to us choosing the toy that we prefer out of the toy box, I'm referring to hundreds of choices of intangible things. Choice is programmed into modern students' lives. Even after they choose the color of their cell phone, the cell phone greets them with more choices.

Those choices are complicated because modern children are always seeking another option for something that is their best fit. This is true of the larger generation and in contrast to the lack of choices that most of us had as children. When many of us were young children, wealth played a significant role in our ability to have choices. Some of our parents did not have the financial means to provide choice and so we worked within the options that we had. Today, more everyday items are geared towards personalization and choice. The Nintendo Switch calls them by name, dolls come with ten changes of clothes and varying hair colors, and their social media pages feed them their interest in high definition.

They are accustomed to options in the academic space. Today's best practices include alternative ways to show mastery. We all know differentiation is every administrator's go-to feedback related to pedagogy practices today. Now, even college access is designed to allow kids to demonstrate their intelligence in multiple ways. The entire world has become more flexible for them and less stringent.

Access-Driven

The internet brought educators and parents alike lots of challenges with withholding information from young people. What used to be housed in alphabetically arranged encyclopedias and libraries is now housed on the internet. I have such fond memories of climbing up onto the computer in my older sister's room after cleaning off the computer disc on my pajama shirt and enduring the ear-numbing sounds of dial-up internet to Ask Jeeves a question. His answers were helpful but then Google came along and the answers became even more accurate. Then YouTube came along, and I no longer had to read about things I was searching for, I could watch a 20-minute video. Then along came Instagram and Tik Tok, and I could watch a two-minute video.

What's even more telling is that now I don't have to find a computer or internet. Nearly all cell phones today have quick access to the internet that brings me information within seconds. That access is liberating for kids and challenging for adults. Kids have access to primary sources all the time whether good or bad for everything they hear adults discussing. It's much harder to shelter them from the world.

Kids love the access that they have to computers. The time frame from wondering to the acquisition of information is short. We use this newfound access in our lessons regularly in lieu of traditional books because we can see the value of this new technology in regard to learning. We bring access into the classroom to create a safe space for learning and to teach students how to use this newfound access. I even remember a time when T.V. programming signed off for the evening; twenty-four hour T.V. is new and they have no idea about that.

Relationally-Driven

There was a day when adults received blind respect, and that wasn't always a good thing. Today, the idea "You have to give respect to get respect" also includes children as recipients of respect. Years ago, that seemed absurd. Today, we recognize that children have boundaries and preferences that should be honored. We also know that, in the past, adults have taken advantage of kids not being able to express boundaries.

Modern kids expect relationships. Their favorite superstars are just a tweet away. They can ask their parents questions any time of the day via cell phones. Even more so, their access to cell phones and chat rooms gives them constant communication with friends and strangers alike. They have questions about the world and receive answers quickly. They play video games on Twitch with strangers around the world that become friends. They regularly receive likes and both positive and negative comments and posts from strangers.

They are constantly in conversation with one another through discord, direct messaging, and any other way they find to communicate. Remember when we used to write to pen pals and had to actually put a letter in the mail and wait two weeks for a response? Remember when our parents answered the phone first and then allowed us to speak to whomever was calling? Remember when we rarely spoke to our friends when we left school? If you have a hard time remembering this, I can guarantee that modern kids don't remember this either.

To clarify, we definitely had relationships with friends. We'd stay outside and play all day with friends, but being respectful to adults was usually our entry to having deep relationships with friends. Today, kids don't experience as many barriers to building relationships. They seek the same sort of access to relationships with adults.

Emotionally Expressive

Today, kids have a voice. Some of that voice is a reflection of social media. If they have something to say they can like a video as a show of agreement, add a positive or negative comment, and receive immediate feedback on those comments. They can even have entire conversations through emojis. Technology allows them to comment as themselves or anonymously with a fake account, which gives them space to be even more expressive. They are constantly able to find validation in their voices. The cartoons and TV shows they watched on Disney and Nickelodeon included extensive dialogue. In stark contrast, we once watched cartoons like Tom and Jerry that had no dialogue.

Many parents have given their children the space to say what they are feeling. Some kids are given the space to yell, use curse words, question their parents, and ask "why" as many times as they need to move forward with what they were asked to do. Again, that has an uncomfortable fit into education.

The language that kids use today with adults is much more informal than when we were young. I was never allowed to use the word "lie." If I suggested that an adult was lying, my grandmother had a conniption! I could not answer adults by saying things like "what" or "hunh." These things were completely off limits and most adults shared those sentiments.

Currently, we acknowledge that children have the same feelings and emotions that we do and that they feel them just as intensely. Those pronounced feelings lead them to speak their minds more with expressive language. They know what they feel and we've told them that we're listening.

It's Going to Be Okay.

It's important to draw an accurate picture of today's young people. It's easy for us to misunderstand them if we only assign negative adjectives to them. Children today are perceptive, inclusive, assertive, inquisitive, creative, and emphatic. We have made a better world for them and they'll continue to make it better like all the generations that have come before them.

When we are the most frustrated, we seem to believe that young people are doomed. That's just not true. There was a time when the elders looked down on the kids who were doing the jitterbug, and the "hippity hop" music was going to ruin us all. Consider the fact that, when young people ushered in civil rights, it wasn't widely accepted by older generations. Now, we can't imagine a world without it. Young people have always pushed society forward, and I know it's tough to accept, but we won't ever be able to bring back the good ol' days.

We also shouldn't define the generation by the most outlandish moments on social media that are shared for the sake of sensationalism. We've all seen the short and extreme clips that garner lots of comments. Most often, we view videos with very little context and these events are not unheard of, but rare. They're often a physical expression of anger that is rooted in some behavior that stemmed from a lack of delicate care by the adults in that child's life. Typically, those kids put on a show for all of the cameras that are on them. I need to tell you that we can't turn back the hands of time. What we can do is care for the kids.

We know that there are many factors contributing to our experience as professional educators today. The COVID pandemic has only exasperated the burnout that many teachers feel. Education has always been a weekend and late night kind of job. But when very little grace was given to teachers when virtual learning was forced upon schools, it didn't feel good. Learning in the moment and on the go while being berated by parents and feeling misunderstood by administrators who had never had to teach in a virtual setting was beating everyone down. Administrators were trying to learn how to run digital schools with some kids in the building and some at home. Parents were trying to understand their students' attention spans and while working from home. Everyone was trying to survive the pandemic despite feelings of fear, the death of loved ones, grief, uncertainty, and limited outlets of peace of joy. We were simply trying to take care of ourselves.

In the next section of this book, we will outline an essential word, "care." Care is missing from the conversation we're having today in education. Taking care of kids today in a school building with so many new dynamics is taxing us all, though we have such big hearts for education. My hope is to help you maintain your heart for education while providing some context on the complexity of care. I can't say enough that I love kids, teachers, school leaders and parents alike. I want our kids to have the best teachers. I believe that's you.

Part II

WHAT IS CARE?

WHAT DOES CARE MEAN, EXACTLY?

*L*ook at each of these guiding sentences.

1. Every day teachers provide <u>care</u> for students during the school day.

2. It was tough to take <u>care</u> of the already fragile and cracked Chromebook.

3. I really <u>care</u> about the students in my class.

These sentences are using the same term "care" but employ different variations of the meaning of the word. Care is a complex word to understand. Searching in any dictionary for the word "care" will bring you to at least four definitions. I've seen as many as ten interpretations for this term. Take a moment to jot down or bring to mind your definition of care.

_____

_____

Now, view this basic dictionary entry.

> *care: n. 1. the provision of what is necessary for the health, welfare, maintenance, and protection of someone or something 2. serious attention or consideration applied to doing something correctly to avoid damage or risk.*
>
> *care: v. 1. feel concern: attach importance to something. 2. look after and provide for the needs of.*

I am certain that what you wrote down matches one of those definitions. More than likely, you may have found yourself jotting down the behaviors of people who care or synonyms for the word care. Care is tough to define on its own, and therein lies the problem.

Care is both a noun and a verb; it's something that we do externally and feel internally. Care is both concrete and abstract. It is both conceptual and tangible. Students, parents, administrators, superintendents, the local news, and state educational officials are all using varying definitions for the word "care." That means we're all miscommunicating when we use the verb and noun "care" interchangeably.

The subject of care is a constant conversation regarding the widespread teacher shortages occurring in the 2020s. The national and political debates about education fill our social media and news feeds. Somewhere in all the chatter, I am certain you have heard nearly all of these sentences:

"These new teachers don't care about kids like they used to."

"Kids just don't care about learning anymore."

"If these kids knew how much I cared about them, they wouldn't be behaving this way."

"These new kids are too much to care for."

"Administrators only care about test scores."

"I don't care about test scores, I want my kids to be actually learning something valuable."

"Parents need to take better care of their kids."

"Kids don't care about authority anymore."

"I don't know how to take care of these kids and take care of myself."

Many of these statements are made in conversation at the height of our emotions when we feel the most frustrated and emotionally drained by a recent experience. The constant intrusive news cycle and notifications that scroll onto our cell phones about school lockdowns and shootings affect us. Even more so, the tendency to attack the educators who are on the frontline with kids every day feels accusatory, repulsive, and inconsiderate. These statements are made in schools, board meetings, PTSA meetings, and teacher happy hours all over the country. It seems that we're all miscommunicating and unsure who to blame as we struggle with taking care of the kids in our modern-day society.

We are looking to hold someone accountable for the social reality that we are all observing. In conversation, my mentor Dr. Michael Gayles refers to this as an invisible enemy. We can't see the real enemies—poverty, racism, sexism, or classism—to hold them accountable. Instead, we see teachers, parents, and administrators as low-hanging fruit to place blame on and to let out frustrations.

Care is subjective. That's why we need to define what we can, especially because everyone seems to be blaming another party for not caring enough. I've seen this scenario many times. A parent of a student says, "You don't even care about my kid." The party that receives these accusatory words is reasonably offended. The list of things they've done for a child rushes back to your memory.

I have been falsely accused of not caring for a student. Once, I gave a student an expensive honey crisp apple that had been in my office refrigerator long enough to develop the perfect temperature and crispness. A few weeks later, that same student's parent gave me an ear-full when I took his bag of hot Cheetos puffs because he was throwing it around the classroom. I was accused of not caring about when kids were hungry. My honey crisp apple that was not purchased on sale says differently (Sorry, I've been holding that in for a while).

Care has a personal interpretation by the receiver. Often when the statement "You don't care about me" is made, the nouns and verbs of its definition are being misused or misheard. An individual is expressing that they have never had an experience of care (verb) being performed by the deliverer of the care and therefore they don't feel care (noun). Let's take a moment to expound on what I mean as I refer to care in this book.

Why Is It Important to Define Care?

At minimum, our basic function in a school is to care for kids. Wait, don't throw your kindle. We're going to unpack care quite a bit. I understand that some may counter and say that our basic function is to educate kids, not care about them. As outlined in *The Heart is Not Enough*, that is no longer true in our modern society. Repeating the wise words of Rita Pearson, "Kids don't learn from people they don't like." I'd venture to add, teachers don't enjoy teaching kids they don't like.

Some educators really care about math, JROTC, language, instilling values into younger generations, or the coveted summer break. Some administrators really care about positions of power, financial success, or being in the room when big decisions are made. At some point, on the day that you're outside of your optimal zone, the emotional burden of caring for kids will show up. Throughout this book, we'll establish the idea that you have to first care for students, then you can teach them math. If you don't care for kids, you're in the wrong profession, especially in today's society. Next, you need some skills.

Many well-meaning educators will say, I love my students. " I would like to push you to rethink the use of the word "love." In actuality, you *care?* You know the sentiment, each school year, you connect with kids for nine months while teaching them reading language arts and then they move on and you do it again. As a school administrator, you work with up to thousands of kids in segments of time, but eventually, they all move on. You may remember some unforgettable kids and funny-spelled names but at some point, if you stay in education long enough, you'll have that dreaded moment.

You're at the gas station and someone comes up to you giddy with glee saying, "Hey Ms. Preyan." You know that you recognize his face and that you've taught him at some point but don't remember his name. Besides, when you taught him he was covered in acne, and here he stands with smooth buttery skin and a deep voice that you don't remember. Beside him are a wife and kids. All of this barely computes in your brain. *Josh has a kid?* This is why I'd argue, we don't *love* kids, we *care* for them. We never forget the people we love.

There are some students that we truly love. We tend to keep up with them over time. We attend their quinceañeras, weddings, baby showers, bat mitzvahs, football games, and any other life events that they invite us to. We typically keep close contact with their parents, and we make it to that weird time when your former student is also an adult and it feels strange that one day you were twelve and twenty-four. You even add them on Facebook when they come of age. The more kids that you love, the better, but at minimum you are charged to care.

Today, as we're seeking to stay afloat in education, care is even more important. In lieu of immediate respect being given to adults, care has become a necessary ingredient in the relationship between teachers and students, parents and schools, teachers, and administrators. We're all asking, "Do you even care about me as a human being?" It's important that we define care because as a friend, Taylor

Lewis, mentioned in a Facebook comment, public education is at risk due to the deep mistrust that is being garnered.

How incredibly scary is it that desperate school districts around the nation are reducing teacher certification requirements to place teachers in classrooms? As true practitioners, we've got to get this right. Why would parents continue to send their students to school with teachers if they hold the belief that educators don't care about their children when there are alternate options? Why would young people enter the teaching profession to be underpaid and unappreciated by society? Why would teachers aspire to leadership roles to be belittled? We all need to prioritize caring for one another.

Throughout this book, I'll operationally share three definitions of care:

1. Care as the act and/or responsibility of supervision. (verb and noun)
2. Care as the act of eliminating further damage or harm. (verb)
3. Care as meaningful interest and thought. (noun verb)

1. Care as the act and/or responsibility of supervision. (noun and verb)

> **Guiding Sentence:** Every day, teachers provide care for students during the school day. (n)
> Teachers care for the students who are in their class. (v)

Referred to as "in loco parentis," schools were originally charged with being the temporary parent of a student in the absence of a parent. At the very minimum, kids are in the care of the school while we educate them. We have a basic responsibility to keep them fed, safe, and warm. I can tell you as a school administrator, if the building is too warm, cold, or meals are unready, lots of calls and decisions are made. If an imminent threat is made to students, schools are required to inform parents and release them safely back into the care of the parents.

Anyone in a school building can share a story with you about someone who didn't do the best job supervising students. I can recall working with substitute teachers who lacked some of the foundational skills of being watchful over students leading to various issues such as fights or theft. Many events that occur in schools can be avoided if the adults accept the charge and responsibility for supervising kids and keeping them safe. Proper supervision creates safety.

Caring for kids looks different with different grade levels of students. Caring for kindergarten students does mean blowing Semaj's nose and tying Harper's shoes. Caring in the upper elementary grades means keeping some deodorant around for Jace, hair gel for La'Daria, and a hairbrush for Phong. Caring at the high school level means staying clear of the student parking lot because Lamar just got his license and the keys to his sister's 2008 Cobalt. In the middle school years, it means keeping a few pads for Marley because inevitably that moment will come. And we secondary folks endure the pungent scent of Axe body spray over body odor. It really stings the nostrils.

Care as the act or responsibility of supervision is the most basic form of care. Nearly any competent adult could care for a child. Caring for a room for twenty-five or more students to teach them computer programming is a bit more complicated. There is a ton of energy in classrooms. Classrooms are a miniature society with cultural systems, traditions, and hierarchies that change from class period to class period. It's amazing how removing one student from a class period can drastically change the culture of that time and place. As educators, we understand that some class periods are easier to care for (remember my beloved terror block). And we either love or loathe the dreaded weeks of testing when we are charged with painstakingly watching students test for hours upon hours. That's just very basic supervision.

Kids need basic supervision because they are exploring the world and often are learning basic boundaries. They need adults who can help them safely navigate the world. They're learning about the social and cultural systems of the world that they were born into. It is, in fact, unsafe to allow Destavion to keep eating glue. Meghan has to be reminded to tie her shoes or she will trip. Davarion needs to be managed as he 3D prints or else he will break the machine and will not have any idea about the value or cost of the machine related to the school budget.

To be clear, schools are not daycares. Teachers are not babysitters, but a basic aspect of care is supervisory. Parents release their sense of worry during the day because they know their kids are learning and safe in the care of the school.

2. Care as the act of eliminating further damage or harm. (verb)

> **Guiding Sentence:** It was tough to take care of the already fragile and cracked Chromebook. (v)

This is the most challenging and intricate type of care to deliver solely because of the wide range of variance that we acknowledge exists in modern children. Caring educators understand that it is our job to care for kids by eliminating the possibility of further damage or harm. My middle school has an animal care club. It is one of my favorite groups to watch. Over the years, we have had chickens, hamsters, fish, guinea pigs, and rabbits. The students were responsible for caring for these animals. Comically and more accurately, their primary function was keeping all of these little creatures alive. They were learning about the complexity of caring for varying fragile items.

Once, the students looked to Youtube to find out if the guinea pigs were male or female and carefully separated them into appropriate cages. A few weeks later, in the middle of world history class, they witnessed the miracle of life as two guinea pigs became seven guinea pigs.

These students were embodying the idea of care while caring for these animals. They learned that the fish were much easier to care for than the guinea pigs. Responsible care requires a gentleness and savviness as you understand the individual needs of the item you are caring for. These students needed to keep a watchful eye over the animals and make constant adjustments. Caring means knowing when to apply what forms of energy and pressure to mitigate damage.

When the chickens were very small, students had to keep them under a light. When the chickens had grown, students were clipping their wings. I can recall watching one of my students, Carl, struggle with clipping the chicken's wings because he was afraid that he would hurt the chicken. When the students needed to bottle feed the baby rabbits, they needed gentler care than when they fed developed rabbits carrots and celery.

This version of care is a verb and is the most tangibly actionable. Students come to us in education in all types of forms. They bring varying traits, patterns, behaviors, and experiences that define how we are to eliminate the possibility of further harm. Let's review some of the variances that define how we seek to eliminate harm and risk in students.

Modern Kids Have Varying Familial Systems

Every student has a distinct home life. Some of those home lives are better than others. The home creates a set of norms in which students operate, and they bring those operational definitions to school with them. Layla may define help as "stand beside me as I learn," while Lauren defines it as "do it for me while I watch." Some ten-year-olds are stricken with responsibility because they're the oldest, yet some ten-year-olds are the spoiled baby who always receives help. Some kids are the oldest and assume responsibility without having to be told and others have to be coached into confidence for small tasks. Whatever the makeup of their home lives, when kids enter a school, they see adults. Their developing mind tells them that these people will, in some form, be a continuation of the norms in which they operate at home. They assume, "These people will take care of me."

Some kids are part of a nuclear family while others come from blended families with multiple step-parents, dads, moms, and sometimes no dad or mom. Some kids are fostered, live with grandparents, and in multigenerational homes. In previous generations, most kids came from a home with a disciplinarian father and a nurturing mother—that was considered balanced. That variance contributes to the behaviors of a student, and it changes our application of care.

Modern Kids Have Varying School-Based Trauma

Before any students step into a school, they've encountered some form of learning. They have experienced someone teaching them to do various things like walking, eating with a spoon, behaving at a restaurant, or using an iPad. As students matriculate through their school years, they develop a love or disdain for school. To paraphrase a very significant body of work, the Matthew Effect refers to a pattern of declining excitement after repeated failure. In education, by the time students reach seventh grade, they know whether or not they will drop out of school.

While students go into kindergarten excited to learn and happy to work with their teacher, this excitement declines as early as second grade. Feelings of comparison to other students and the perception that their teacher does not enjoy working with them or feels frustrated working with them contribute to this gradual decline of school interest. Students happily transition to middle school hoping to feel something different but can be met with the same feelings and barriers. By seventh grade, students could feel that school is not a place of success for them.

As students have varying levels of success with educational and social aspects of school, they draw conclusions about their math, reading, physical prowess, and behavioral skills based on their history with school. They understand which types of teachers they tend to get along with. Of course, they have preferences between the lunchroom's chicken nuggets and pizza.

It's important to note that many students have a distrusting relationship with school based on the experiences they've had in specific schools and with adults whom they felt didn't do their best caring for them. That variance contributes to how we eliminate further risk or damage to them. The needs of a student that is struggling with perfectionism are different from a student who is struggling with low confidence. The same is true of a student who struggles with humanities as opposed to math and science.

Modern Kids Have Varying Interests

Kids have a wide range of interests. Great educators will often survey students on the first day of school to learn about their interests and goals. At my current campus, we survey kids on what they believe their superpowers are, and students would ultimately share their interests with us. Their answers ranged from Joe's love of polytechnic fire, Calin's love of horses, Issac's love of cattle, Elsabet's love for makeup, to kids who had absolutely no idea what they were interested in. Often, school clubs are a representation of what students are interested in outside of school.

In our contemporary day of technology and the video-sharing social media site Tik Tok (which will probably be a funny joke in the future as is myspace and AOL messenger chat), kids are exposed to many things. Kids have access to quality education at their fingertips. As a young person, my options for learning about foreign ideas were the encyclopedia, asking Jeeves when my older sisters got off of the phone line that was the critical component to our dial-up internet, asking an adult, or stumbling upon someone who had experience with something that was of interest to me. Today, kids can think of anything and type it into YouTube, TikTok, or Instagram and have knowledge about their interests. Even more so, their home pages are then curated towards their interests.

I can recall a student telling us his superpower was military-grade machine rifles. His dad was stunned and didn't know how to support or care for his son's interests without posing a risk to others. Gratefully, we were able to steer the interest in a positive direction when he discovered robotics and the various items we had in our school maker space. All of these items contribute to the variance within kids that we consider as we seek to eliminate further risk or damage to them.

Modern Kids Have Varying Defense Mechanisms

Many of the behaviors that challenge educators are defense mechanisms that kids have developed to steer themselves away from trouble or protect themselves when they feel harmed. That is complicated because sometimes those behaviors are combative and feel disrespectful. They trigger us because we're human, too.

When some kids feel threatened, they yell at adults, they pick on other kids to increase their self-esteem, and they escape by leaving classrooms. Sometimes kids fight because they are so angry inside at invisible opponents that a tangible enemy feels conquerable. Kids can be neglected and cling to adults in the school building that make them feel loved as opposed to attending class. We have to coach those behaviors to mitigate potential harm to those students today or later in life. Admittedly, those behaviors largely contribute to the emotional burnout that we feel. Frankly, education programs don't teach you how to navigate those moments. And as humans, those behaviors leave us with feelings about our own selves; somehow, we're just supposed to keep teaching polynomials.

Let's Recap

With such varying home lives, interests, goals, and school experiences, mitigating the option for further damage to students is layered. We have to pay attention to students. We can't determine what their needs are if we don't consider all the ways in which we could know them. Students are delicate and we receive them as they are—in a state of innocence. As we perform our job as educators, we are hoping at best to not cause further damage. If a student struggles with a science concept, we don't want to cause further damage to that. If they are ignored at home, we should not reinforce the feeling that they are unimportant. If they experience a level of shyness that is rooted in a lack of acceptance, we should not reinforce the practice of hiding their intelligence for social acceptance.

I know you may be thinking, "I'm a teacher, not a therapist. Asking me to fix these things for a child is an insurmountable task." To be piercingly clear, caring for kids doesn't mean fixing these things, it means considering them.

3. Care as meaningful interest and thought (verb)

> **Guiding Sentence:** It is important that teachers care about kids. (v)

As a young child, I loved the experience of learning with a warm soul directing a group. Whether this experience was the result of Vacation Bible School, summer camp, choir, school, or learning from my older siblings, it filled me up. The experience of a kind, friendly, smiling, human pouring into a young person is a social rite of passage in American life. It's a life experience that is due and coveted for young children. Elementary school teachers are reasonably cheerful and bubbly as they lay the foundation in the minds of young people that school is good. We teach children that school is a safe, happy place that will take care of you and grow you away from the safety of the home that you know. Imagine being ripped away from home at four years old to spend your day with cold, non-expressive adults.

Many of us who really care about kids have had similar positive experiences at some point in our trajectory in school. Whether it was our middle school dance teacher, high school JROTC instructor, lunch lady, or middle school principal, our minds have made a positive correlation with school because of those individuals. Our fond memories of the place and people who poured so deeply into us make us want to care *for* kids. School is a symbol of connection to those fond memories and people who started us on a path of benevolence in life.

"Care" as meaningful interest is the warm and fuzzy feelings that we all traditionally associate with caring. It's what we say so passionately when we are angry with systems of power and administration that don't seem to understand the weight of the challenges we feel in education. "The people who make these tests don't care about these kids." "These kids don't know how much I care about them."

"Care" as meaningful thought is a deep internal commitment to kids that many educators feel. Education comes with serious challenges. We agree to work with large numbers of kids that aren't ours to prepare them to be a part of the larger world. We wake up early, spend our own money, spend time away from our own families, and accept measly salaries while doing work that will never be properly compensated because the contribution to society is beyond financial value. Most educators have lives that have cultivated them towards education.

As I shared in the preface, my elementary school and my grandmother deeply shaped my views on education. Without question, I grew up in a rich society of values that existed within a two-mile radius by Greenfield and Eight Mile on the west side of Detroit. My siblings, who were twenty years my senior, and I shared school teachers. Those teachers, who had married and no longer carried their maiden names, had gracefully aged and were connected to our larger community. They had what we call "street credit." The teachers in my elementary school saved the community I grew up in and sustained our section of the city with their wisdom and grace. I was cared for in meaningful ways as a student, and that gave me a love for education.

I was a future teacher for Ms. Woodall in the fifth grade which meant I was able to leave class ten minutes early to erase and clean her chalkboard. I coveted the experience of grading papers using that old-school green cardboard tool that you had to slide to give the percentage correct.

Then, when I was in the sixth grade, I had an opportunity to work in the main office as an office assistant. Man! This was the highest honor. I got to go into the office of Shirley Daggs-Monroe, my elementary school principal who referred to me affectionately as "Namesake." It makes perfect sense that I did absolutely nothing with my journalism degree; I was always meant to be in a school. Very few of us stumble into education.

Admittedly, I am the educator who has a hard time turning it off. When I go to the grocery store, I tell kids to stop running. I find myself making sure kids don't skip the line at the waterpark, and I am a sucker for a kid selling water on the side of the road. I care about kids. I like kid-movies, Hot Cheetos, and in the words of so many kids when I meet them, "You have teacher vibes." A form of being a caring educator is liking kids.

The commitment of an educator is professionally unmatched. In yesteryear, working on the weekends, through holidays, and summer training wasn't just a set of unspoken educational rules, it was expected. We've changed quite a bit, but there was a time when you weren't a team player if you didn't work Saturday School for free. Even the summer months were spent preparing for the school year as teachers hoarded spirals, composition notebooks, pencils, scissors, and glue. Most teachers have such a deep commitment to kids that they understand the strange conundrum that exists with pay and commitment. If teachers received the salary they deserved some people would abuse this sacred career. Some teachers would do this job no matter the pay.

Now, I have to take a moment to say that as a society we have necessarily removed the idea that free labor is admirable when you can not pay your basic bills. The compensation of teachers has been lacking for too long and as new generations come into the profession, they are demanding that teachers be able to make a living wage. This shift is necessary because teachers should not be poor.

Care as meaningful thought is intangible but it is what guides us to persevere. We love the profession because we understand that we serve kids and this society. Many of us see education as a passion, ministry, or life's calling.

Now What?

To recap, I've outlined what I operationally mean when I say "care."

1. Care is supervision.

2. Care is eliminating further risk or harm.

3. Care is meaningful thought.

The source of some of our emotional burnout, fatigue, and frustrations in education is that, as an entire society, we are learning how to care for modern kids. We would love to only teach kids conduction and density, but as it turns out, we have to care for them first. Care is complex, but now what?

Some aspects of care as supervision are inherent. If you put an adult in a room with children, that adult will naturally begin to care for them because kids are innocent and inexperienced in life. Some aspects of care such as removing the risk of damage are also inherent. If you gave a small child an egg, something in them would make them move a little slower, understanding that the egg is delicate and can break. We all have something in this world that we care about in terms of meaningful thought. Care, in its basic form, can be inherent because it is a matter of the heart, but it is still a skill that can be cultivated.

I believe there are key behaviors that caring educators engage in that should be brought to the front of our understanding. These behaviors are not exhaustive, and I am certain that as I continue to work with kids, more behaviors will come to the forefront. But, this list of behaviors ensures that all kids who are in a school building are properly cared for. These behaviors are the foundation of someone who knows how to build responsible relationships with kids as a caring adult and focus on the behaviors of modern students.

This book is not about classroom management. It's not about social-emotional learning. It's not about circles or restorative discipline. It's not about schoolwide discipline. It's not about coaching teachers who are struggling with connecting with students. The basis of so many school strategies assumes that the strategy is being delivered by a caring adult who knows how to care for kids.

This book is for anyone who is ever charged with caring for kids. You may find yourself at times struggling and have no idea why it seems you're struggling to supervise a group, mitigate additional risk to kids, or feel meaningful connections with kids. View these next eleven behaviors as a checklist for yourself to ensure that these things aren't getting in the way. Some of these stories will be comical and they may take you back to similar instances you have encountered in education. Laugh a little. Be honest with yourself. If something hurts you, say, "Ouch."

I don't share these tips from a place of perfection. I share them from a place of lessons. Each time that I struggled with a specific student I reminded myself that I *cared about* them and so I needed to do a better job *caring for* them.

Part 3

HABITS OF EDUCATORS WHO CARE FOR MODERN KIDS

HABITS OF EDUCATORS WHO CARE FOR MODERN KIDS

*E*ducation is a public service. In some form, we will always be adapting to the changes of society. Public school for all children is barely 100 years old and the integration of schools is less than 70 years old. There have been many historical moments that have brought political pressure into schools. Imagine the emotional complexity of being a teacher during integration in the South on either side of the table as we tread into new social waters. Imagine the historical, necessary discomfort and how far we have come since those days (and how far we still have left to go).

Consider the fears of being a teacher during the rise of divorce, women entering the workforce, or times of war. Everything that our society had known about women being home to care for the children was being revolutionized.

Imagine being a teacher during one of the nearly 900 teacher strikes that have occurred in our history. Or during the period when it was believed that teachers should not be married. For centuries we've been wondering, "If we make these changes, will the kids be alright?" Teachers have always been public-facing figures, and education has always been on the front page of the newspaper.

Today, as an American society we are facing many challenges that have reasonably affected our schools. There has been a great resignation, a worldwide pandemic, calls for inclusivity, challenges to appropriate curriculum, the onset of acknowledging mental health concerns in children, and political dissonance. There are debates about school funding, restrooms, critical race theory, and teacher compensation.

The world is debating the relevance of the five-day work week and wondering why professionals should not be able to work from home and create more flexible schedules that work for their lives. The metaverse is looming as children are born into digital realities and maybe one day students won't even step into a school building, ever. I want to apologize because I don't have the answer to any of those things. There is much time spent on the commentary of those issues because they are quite complex. Very few of those very real issues can be changed in one moment, with one book, or with one singular decision.

The habits listed in the next few pages won't fix any of those problems. These habits are about lessening the emotional burnout caused by caring for kids in our modern-day society. Just to recap, in our modern day, we have placed a new emphasis on emotional intelligence. Our relationship with children today feels more challenging than ever before because the version of what it means to respect adults has evolved. With all of the constant change, the challenge of learning, in the moment, how to care for modern children is emotionally taxing. As we all wade through the waters of survival mode, caring for kids is complicated when you are caring for yourself.

As a school administrator, every day brought me a new challenge. One day, a cat was running through the school. The next day, there was a full-on girl drama. In most cases, the first time I encountered an issue, I didn't have the language or skillset to pull from to navigate the scenario. Like most of us, I fell into old habits or overcompensated with the skills that I did have. These next pages aim to magnify the lessons I have learned from each of these complicated scenarios. These skills affirm students as humans and you as a caring educator. These habits also seek to ensure that students are properly supervised, that we do no additional harm to them, and that we operate from a place of meaningful interest in their lives. They aim to assist you in your locus of control.

As I have gained new learning over my years in education, I was able to mitigate some of the emotional impact of these scenarios because there was something for me to pull from. Often when I had no idea how to approach a specific conversation with a parent or stakeholder, I would ask my principal or a trusted colleague for language. Not knowing what to say would put me in a state of overthinking.

Again, I am certain that you're reading this book because you are a passionate educator that cares for kids. I am even more certain that you already do some of these things and I hope these pages bring you perspective as to why they work. I feel a sense of vulnerability sharing these embarrassing stories. Keep an open mind. These stories that I share are true and from a true practitioner who understands the burdens and barriers that we are all feeling. I hope that you laugh, just a little, and feel a sense of solidarity in knowing someone gets it.

SEE INVISIBLE KIDS

*C*aring for kids means caring for all kids. I'm intentionally choosing to start here because we tend to forget about such a large number of students who come to school every day giving their absolute best. They aren't loud, screaming for help, or boisterous, but they are many other things.

They are artistic, shy, helpful, self-disciplined, bashful, never make a fuss, come from loving humble families, and are always willing to grow. No matter how many times you tell them to take the absence notes to the office, they always give them to you because they trust you more than the lady in the office (and they're probably a little scared of her).

They draw you pictures for your birthday, ask if you were sick when you missed a day of school, notice your new haircut, and always wear their uniform. They offer to buy you lunch because they have $20 today and you were the first person they thought of. Of course, they need you to use your 30-minute duty-free lunch to go buy the food, but the main goal is to buy you lunch.

They are the silent wheel in education that we don't pay enough attention to. They deserve the same space in our hearts and minds as the more challenging moments with students that drain our energy. When the school yearbook comes out, they search for themselves in the shadows of the athletes, cheerleaders, class clowns, class presidents, and the class couple. I'm challenging all educators to have a stronger commitment to those kids. They, too, are deserving of our think pieces and initiatives. They are rarely in our conversations.

I've been guilty of allowing a few students to define how I feel about all kids. Unfortunately, we tend to lose our passion due to less than five percent of our kids while temporarily forgetting the needs and importance of the larger 95%. We allow a small group to consume our minds and hijack our emotions on tough days. When we allow some students to deplete our emotional capacity, it disregards the other students and leaves their needs unmet. When our bucket is empty from a few kids, we don't have anything left to pour into the remaining students. I've had moments when I felt poorly about myself when I berated my class as a whole for the actions of a few. I can admit that my lack of skill in working with specific students made me feel a sense of failure sometimes. I can be honest with myself about that. My absolute favorite thing is when we cancel the school dance because three kids were talking when we asked two hundred to be silent (we know good and well that the dance is not canceled).

I know. I can hear you. It's the administrator's job to deal with difficult students. The culture of a school should not allow any deviations from the rules. This book isn't about blaming anyone for anything. It's about sharing the best habits of practice. I'll share more about this later. For now, keep an open mind.

Let's be honest, some kids are easier to care for in terms of supervision and they have less behaviors or defense mechanisms that challenge or trigger us. Amanda was an extremely sweet kid. She was unusually short and always helpful. One day she came to my office crying. Jackson had taken her glasses again.

"Why do you keep giving him your glasses?"

"Because he asked for them."

"Amanda, you don't have to give your things to him just because he asked."

I sat in the office and practiced saying "no" with her for about fifteen minutes. In the hallway, we practiced again, "Amanda, give me your book bag."

"...No..." she said with uncertainty.

A few weeks later, she was saying no to everyone. Still doing so with bashfulness in her voice, but nevertheless, trying. She deserves the same fifteen minutes as the student who stuffed a chicken nugget into a barbeque sauce container and chucked it across the room during your lesson on US presidents.

Before Amanda came to my office that day, I rarely noticed her. She was never sticking out asking for attention. I wondered how many moments I may have missed when she needed help, but I was too drained to notice. I watched Amanda grow into a more confident tween, and I began to call on her to help me with more things. It was just a way of making her feel seen. She is still pretty bashful but has slightly more of a voice. She deserves that. Every kid deserves that.

How Does Seeing Invisible Kids Demonstrate Care?

When we care for kids, we commit to removing the risk of additional harm. It is neglectful of me to watch Amanda engage in this behavior without taking a moment to intervene. I have to consider what it means for the rest of her life that she struggles to say "no." Jackson was a cool, popular kid who was socially mature. She didn't feel very worthy when she encountered him because he was more socially advanced, and she was quite the rule follower. I cared for Amanda, and it was my job to teach her anything that I could as an adult with some level of wisdom on how being a doormat could affect her later in life.

Allowing ourselves to be governed by the narrative that all of the kids are out of reach depletes us before we've even had a chance to begin our impact. Make it a habit when you wake up in the morning to think of all the kids. Not just some. We come into the building with the expectation that a certain kid will engage in the behavior that challenges us. I did. I could tell how my day was going to progress based on the way that I interacted with a certain student at uniform check in the morning. And shortly after, one of those really sweet kids would say something that filled my cup with joy and reminded me of my purpose. Search for the space to contribute to the kids who show up every day ready to learn.

Some kids are simpler to supervise. Some kids exhibit traditional qualities that resonate with us. They display traits that we immediately understand as respect and this makes us more willing to show care for them.

As educators, many of us are guilty of referring to a specific class period or grade level as the "good class." Most times what we really mean is, these kids are the most obedient. They are quiet, they don't push back, and they don't make me feel challenged. Because these students don't tend to push us, we don't push ourselves to reach them. Imagine receiving less because you are obedient.

Even the "good students" notice that the more outspoken or challenging students are commanding the teacher's attention and leaving them neglected. At times, we even notice large academic gaps in these students but pass them on because they're sweet kids as opposed to taking an additional moment to invest in their academic success.

It is perfectly fine that those students have a healthy relationship with authority. Many of them have parents who have raised them to be respectful and kind—they shouldn't be punished or overlooked because of that. Caring for boys and girls means caring for all kids. As your day will allow, find meaningful ways to connect with those students to make them feel worthy of your energy.

Keeping these kids in mind reminds us of the entire picture of the students we serve. I've seen teachers have moments of deep joy interacting with students who are unseen by others. Every student in our building is in our care and we should have strong commitments to each of them. We can't handpick the students who come into our schools each year, but we can be conscious of where we focus our attention.

We can't mitigate harm for kids that we don't know. Caring means having meaningful interest and that takes some conversation and more intimate experiences with kids we don't normally go out of our way to spend time with, whether that's academic or social.

Lastly, modern students are relational. Consider what it means that we don't take the time to develop relationships with these students. These students can also seek solace in dangerous online outlets because suddenly they feel seen. The access that online media provides can be both liberating and dangerous for young impressionable minds that are looking for friendship. We can't continue to ignore these kids.

Care Tips

1. Students we overlook are not all introverted. Sometimes you will discover an incredibly vibrant personality.

2. Initially, approach kids who are typically shyer in one-on-one opportunities or when they are with trusted friends.

3. Make positive phone calls home.

4. Engage their parents in conversation to ask their parents about what they want to be true for them. For example, their parents may need help with pulling them out of their shell.

5. Notice the small things to build a relationship with them (drawings, poems, new hairdos, characters on their keychains, screensavers, etc...).

6. Communicate with their parents about notable moments and gaps that you notice both academic and social.

Improvisational Language

1. What's something that makes you happy?

2. Tell me something that's really important to you?

3. I apologize, I really want to know your name. Do you mind telling me?

4. I'm sorry, I was serving that other student. Is it okay if I make some time for you now?

5. Is there something that you want to say out loud?

6. Did I forget to include you?

7. Is there a better way for us to communicate? Whether that's a written note, email, or a Google Doc?

8. Do you need translation help from someone that you trust?

9. What do you need to be comfortable right now?

LISTEN, THEN REDIRECT

Carter was two parts compliant and two parts disobedient. She had a kind heart and always wanted to assist where she could. The only problem was that she preferred to assist and serve our school community during the time that she should have been in class. Each day, she never wanted to attend her morning advisory class. She had a contentious relationship with her morning teacher and knew that she often triggered her into a downward spiral of a day. She knew enough about herself to understand that starting her day in a combative way with her teacher wasn't productive for her. Each morning, she would ask me if there were tasks that she could complete to avoid going to her morning course.

Many mornings I listened to her while we took the long route to her morning advisory class. She would share a myriad of things on those morning walks. She told me about her adoption, love interest, friendship dynamics, grievances with her younger sister, and her opinions on the world. In addition, she would say negative things about her teacher; I would only listen, never validating or agreeing. She would tell me about how she was not going to a specific teacher's class later in the day and again, I would only listen.

The wisdom that we have as adults understands that sometimes humans are just venting. When she would finally stop talking or we'd arrive at the door, I would redirect her.

"I'll come visit you in Ms. So and So's class later today."

She would walk in the room and say, "Okay!"

Most often, she was never serious about what she was expressing, she just wanted someone to talk to. When I met her in the other class, I would give her a gentle pat on the back, a smile, or a starburst (educators know how much kids love a random starburst or jolly rancher).

How Does Listening Then Redirecting Demonstrate Care?

I learned that there were some invaluable exchanges during those listening sessions. When Carter was her most defiant and no one could get through to her, she then would listen to me. Carter was strong-willed and determined. When she felt threatened or uncared for, she became her most defiant. With all of the things she shared with me on our walks, I knew some of the places that her strong-willed nature came from. When the moment came, the equity of listening to her made it easier to redirect her when necessary. The power dynamic of "because I said so" works differently for her. It worked because I, the one who listens to you when you need an ear, said so.

Modern children voice their opinions more openly. They are raised in the age of opinion and personalization. Though I listened, my redirection was always matter-of-fact, such as, "I'll come see you in class later today." Listening does not always mean that you agree with a student's statements.

Caring for boys and girls means lending a safe ear. These relational kids need someone who will willingly listen without judgment but with wisdom. A twelve-year-old is still learning about the world. Kids draw conclusions about the world based on the limited knowledge they have. Also, kids need to be redirected when they are wrong. Even as adults, we understand that sometimes we don't like feedback from people with whom we don't feel a connection.

Listening without judgment, but with wisdom, is a moment to hear their interests and learn what they're still making sense of in this complicated world. While listening is the basis of strong relationship building, listening then redirecting is a component of strong, relational discipline. You're able to inventory pieces of the conversation for equity at a later date when you need to work with the student when they're not at their emotional best.

When children tell you what they won't do and you have a positive relationship with them, something stops them in their tracks. Many of us have had this moment: a student is walking away from you as you give them reasonable and correct instructions. See that student in all of his glorious insubordination standing underneath the Michael Jordan inspirational poster in the hallway with the pencil-drawn mustache, reinforced by an expo marker.

If you're like me, sit with that trigger for a moment. The best disciplinarians have a control in their voices that says, "Come back here, now." That works in most scenarios. When you're working with a student who needs more delicate care, it's much more complicated. Some students want to see if they can win the battle with you and so they take a moment to compete. They will pause and look at you deep into your eyes to determine if this will be the day that they finally win the battle with authority.

We've discussed that some kids have immediate respect for authority that is instilled in them for various reasons that can be socially and developmentally appropriate. An appropriate response to authority is a part of our society. Oppositional defiance is considered a disability that is protected by Section 504 of the IDEA Act and should be taken seriously. However, kids still need to be redirected when they are wrong. Kids are just more prone to listen to someone who has supported them. Listening to kids only costs us time and a small piece of our pride, but the dividends are highly profitable.

As a school administrator, I am called to many scenarios in which a teacher and a student are in disagreement. In every instance, my first job is to listen to both the student and the teacher. Oftentimes, I hear kids say, "He wouldn't even listen to me." As a young person myself, I was required to do whatever the adult told me, and sometimes the adult was wrong. In the words of every child, ever, "That's not fair." It doesn't feel good to be blamed for something that you didn't do or to feel that your intentions were misunderstood.

Again, modern kids are relationally driven. When they feel as though you won't listen, they express that frustration. We know how expressive their language can be as they repeat phrases they've heard from us or others. Listening first invites relationships. It does not mean students won't have consequences.

When we listen to kids, we can correct them in a way that resonates with them because we know them. As educators, we are working with large groups of children at a time. We don't have as much intimate time with each student to be able to listen to their inner thoughts. Favorably, humanities teachers of reading and social studies tend to listen to students structurally in their lessons because we read students' inner thoughts in their writing and discuss their opinions on the lives of characters or historical events. Teachers of other content areas have to create meaningful moments to listen to kids. Nonetheless, listening pays equity in the most meaningful moments.

Care Tips

1. Use warm language to show that you were listening.

2. Use repetitive, concise language to redirect.

3. Over-communicate the redirection.

4. Inventory pieces of the conversation for later dates and times.

5. When listening, assume that the conversation is confidential.

6. If you can't listen at that moment, offer them a later time to circle back to the conversation.

Improvisational Language

1. I'm listening.

2. Am I missing something?

3. Is there something that I need to know?

4. I heard you when you said ____, and you're missing _____. What do you think about what I've just added to what you shared with me?

5. It's important for me to understand what you're trying to share with me. Right now, I can't listen. Do you feel okay with heading to class and me coming to get you a little later to listen to you?

6. Am I asking the wrong questions?

BE CONSISTENT WHEN IT HURTS

*S*ome of the students with whom I've had the most challenges needed the most consistency. Carl was the most layered child I have ever met. He loved animals, was perceptive and funny. Additionally, he had a varying range of disabilities from ADHD, to emotional disturbances, and undiagnosed signs of autism that presented challenges beyond the classroom. He loved animals, video games and was funny, emotional, sensitive, child-like, and of course, insubordinate.

We had a demerit system that required him to attend detention when he received three demerits. Most Fridays, I did not want to stay for detention, but this was something that worked for him. He hated detention because he had to stay after school. At times he would run to his bus to avoid detention, and sometimes he would sit in detention and disrupt or pass the time. I was even required to give him accommodations during detention according to his IEP. Each time, if he did not finish his detention assignment, I would tell him when it needed to be finished, and I would pick it up from his house Saturday morning.

This was not my favorite thing at all. I did not want to drive to his home on an educator's beloved Saturday morning to pick up a detention assignment from a student, but I had no choice. I had to be consistent. If I told him there would be detention, it had to happen. If I said he had an hour to complete something, it had to be. And when he asked, "What happens if I don't..." I had to deliver on the promise every single time. It hurt.

I had to do this for a handful of students. I can recall going to pick up a detention assignment once, and the family closed the blinds and turned off the lights to avoid me. I've done this for many students, never wavering. It hurt me but helped them. It also built the necessary trust in the relationship. Kids accepted that there would be a consequence and it was not personal.

Admittedly and embarrassingly, consistency is not my strong suit. In fact, it's my Achilles heel; however, it was a central skill that I had to develop when working with modern kids. When I would see a student regress, I could identify my inconsistency with the student. I'd promise to call home and forget or it would slip my mind to add them to the detention list. Consistency is a disciplinary skill that needs some space to be bent but not to waver. Fun fact: the strongest and tallest buildings are required to waver to withstand storms and weathering.

Let's be honest, when we were kids, we tried to get away with lots of things. There was a time when I believed my grandmother had some sort of x-ray vision and could see us all the way down the street. Turns out, our neighbors were just letting her know what we were doing, including the time we were throwing rocks at cars.

Today, there tends to be a bit more skepticism when we share with a parent a challenging behavior in which a student has engaged. The neighbors aren't watching as much. It feels like kids win in those moments, and that doesn't feel good for us when our intentions are good. Again, it feels like no one trusts our judgment as professional educators.

I am not advising you to spend your Saturday going to students' homes. In fact, my failure to be consistent during the school day and earlier in the school year is what required me to have to take such extreme measures. I had to work much harder to prove that I could be consistent because I had not been. Many difficult moments with students were my fault. Kids don't operate with the same "yes sir" mentality, and we can fill the gap with consistency.

Kids know which educators are consistent. It's the only teacher that they do homework for. It's the only teacher that they tuck in their shirt for. We are all consistent in some way, just not necessarily in a positive productive way. Some of us consistently respond to students with empty promises and consequences that we can't deliver. Kids learn from inconsistency, too.

Because modern kids are emotionally expressive, they'll give you feedback on your ability to be consistent. I've been the receiver of, "You didn't say anything last time," comments. Ouch. Allowing a child to engage in unproductive behavior repeatedly without intervening isn't delivering responsible care.

I was hoping to teach Carl that there are consequences for his actions. Instead, I taught him that sometimes there are consequences for your actions. I made working with him harder than it needed to be. Of course, it triggered me when he responded to my inconsistencies. I was working so hard, but it wasn't working. Because I had a relationship with Carl, it left me even more emotionally scarred because I thought the relationship was the central disciplinary tool. It's not. The relationship is part of the foundation, but the house is built from my repeated use of strong tools to teach students appropriate behavior.

How Does Showing Consistency When It Hurts Demonstrate Care?

We've all had an experience in life where a consequence is delayed and it felt like we'd gotten away with it. We know that we haven't. Even more so, we tend to repeat the behavior more often because we've taught ourselves that it's okay. Eventually, whatever consequence is waiting for us is coming, and it'll sting even more due to its delay. Kids are no different. Consequences are about learning.

Many kids who have behavioral challenges appear unruly but, in reality, they are engaging in normal behaviors that are uncoached. As wise caring adults, we can identify that and assist them on their journey in life. Sometimes we tend to forget that kids have only been operating on their own ideas and patterns for a short amount of years. Especially in comparison to the context we have in the world. Our first response to a student's misbehavior is the most important as it sets the tone for how they believe you are allowing them to operate in the culture of your class.

Care Tips

1. Use concise language in every interaction that is related to discipline.

2. Use the same language each time.

Ex. Today, I need you to attend every class. Later that day: "How many classes have you attended?" At the end of the day: "Today, you attended every class; that is what I asked for."

3. Repeat the concise language to the parent in every interaction so that they can support you.

4. Don't assume that the parent is unable to assist. Work together to create a common goal. If the parent is unavailable, over-communicate the asks that you have.

5. Ask a staff member or trusted colleague to call you out when you aren't being consistent.

6. Align your language amongst the students, administrators, fellow teachers, and parents.

7. Ask the student to repeat back to you the action you are requesting.

8. Use a behavior tracker with the same language.

9. Limit progress to no more than three accurate goals at a time.

10. Own when you haven't been consistent.

11. If you find yourself being inconsistent, go back and correct yourself immediately.

Improvisational Language

1. When you _____, I will _____.

2. If you aren't able to _____, then I will _____.

3. Let me repeat that.

4. Sometimes the answer is yes and sometimes the answer is no. Right now, the answer is no.

SET BOUNDARIES IN THE RELATIONSHIP

As a first-year teacher, I related to the students on a personal level. I was a twenty-three-year-old, first-year teacher and they were thirteen. I was more similar to them than I was to the 60-year-old teacher across the hall. Josue was an artistic, relational, goofy kid. On this particular day, he was really unfocused. He was his most social, and I could tell when he came in the room that he was going to be tough to reel in.

As I tried my best to teach the class, he picked up the yardstick. "Ms., you need to get these kids in line." He wailed the yardstick around, smacking it on various desks as he paced up and down the rows. Of course, this was my beloved eighth-period class that you've already read so much about. His energy was infectious, and the rest of the class was starting to be pulled into his cosmic energy. He was loaded with a charisma that resonated with both the girls and the boys, and he knew that. He was a natural galvanizer of people.

I had too personal of a relationship with Josue. He saw me as his friend. Josue was not wrong for seeing me as a friend. It was my place to reposition myself in his life as a caring, safe adult, not a friend. "Friend" is the best word that kids know, and they attribute the term to people with whom they feel safe. Well, on that day I learned a tough lesson about having boundaries with kids.

Josue smacked me on the bottom with the yardstick that he had been wailing around. Yes, you read that correctly. I was in a state of shock and embarrassment for a moment. The kids in class looked on wondering what was next. This was more than a first for me. As a first-year teacher, I felt completely incompetent. I can guarantee there is nothing in any teacher education program that prepares you for this moment. Most training programs won't tell you that this was the result of my failure to properly care for Josue. I blurred the line with Josue to connect with him.

I asked Josue to step into the hallway and call his mother. I asked him to tell his mother what occurred in his own words. He was reasonably shaking and stuttering. His mother had a hard time even understanding his words because they seemed so far-fetched. He was embarrassed and so was I. However, this was ultimately my failure to properly care for him by setting proper boundaries. I was absolutely certain that I was going to be fired that day. I never told my principal this happened (sorry, Mr. Parker).

As a school administrator, I've seen these scenarios many times with kids and teachers. What starts as a meaningful connection between a student and a trusted teacher gets skewed when the student crosses a boundary that was never placed. It opens the door for events like the one that occurred with Josue.

When I was young, I never had a personal, informal conversation with my teachers. There was an invisible line that we were to never cross. Today, we are more open to being seen as layered humans, but we also know kids can ask some strange questions. One time, when I was eight months pregnant, I went into the health classroom while students were learning about reproductive health. You should have seen some of the looks that I got. In those instances, kids are learning what's appropriate and what's not. It's our job to help them understand how to interact with others and how to respect an individual's physical and conversational boundaries. Because I was the school administrator, they didn't ask me any questions directly, but they kept glancing at me with each new detail that they learned about reproduction. If they would have asked questions of me, I would have given them coaching on boundaries or redirected them to a more appropriate conversation.

How Does Setting Boundaries Demonstrate Care?

Josue was exploring many things in his life, and one of those was the relationship he had with authority and adults. He was interested in things that were not appropriate for a child, and I was a caring adult who needed to teach him. He was interested in me as a human. I was young and his favorite teacher. He didn't ask the same questions to all his teachers. But eliminating harm meant creating a necessary boundary that I found hard to learn how to manage.

Modern kids are relational and are born into the days of access—that includes access to you. They want to know things about you because information is rarely withheld from them. "Grown-folks business" doesn't apply to a generation that can watch your Instagram stories at two a.m. I've had students comment, like, or find videos of me online from over ten years ago. Though I was offended at times, I learned to create a teachable moment.

Kids often strike up lots of harmless conversation. There isn't anything wrong with a student sharing with you that she likes Jason from third-period Chemistry. It's also okay just to listen. Teachers should provide appropriate guidance that eliminates the risk of harm but doesn't invite what feels like friendship to students. When students talk with their teachers about relationships, it is often a moment to hear about how they think about appropriate boundaries and their wild misconceptions regarding loyalty (If you know, you know).

I've seen kids debate whether or not their boyfriend or girlfriend should have the password to each other's social media sites and if they should be able to read all of their messages. As adults, we know how harmful that thinking is. We should take that moment to teach and mentor, not to build a casual bond.

Care Tips

1. Always use discernment in your interactions with students.

2. Be the holder of the line, don't depend on kids for that.

3. Consult your school counselor or a trusted colleague if you are unsure about whether a boundary has been crossed.

4. If it seems wrong, it probably is.

5. If you aren't comfortable telling a parent that you had this conversation with their child, it's likely inappropriate.

Improvisational Language

1. Hey, this isn't an appropriate conversation for you and me. Is there a friend that you can share this with?

2. This is a delicate topic, are you seeking guidance or just someone willing to listen?

3. Before you continue, is this something that you would be comfortable with someone else knowing? I may not be able to keep this conversation private.

4. I love chatting with you, but I need to change the subject.

HIDDEN HABIT

Don't keep secrets.

There are times when a student will ask you to keep a secret. This is different from setting a boundary for kids and halfway to our next habit, connecting with parents. When a student asks you to keep their secret, they are likely vulnerable and see you as a safe adult that they trust. Still, you can't promise a kid that you will keep their secret.

Over my years in education, kids have shared many things with me in confidence. Some things weren't very salacious. One student shared with me that she didn't like cheese and didn't understand all the hype around it. As a Mexican American, I can understand why not liking cheese was a cultural faux–pas as cheese is a key ingredient in Mexican cuisine. Some students only shared thoughts of them exploring their sexual orientation or about stealing from their great-grandpa's quarter collection.

In contrast, some of the things that kids shared with me I was obligated to share with protective services. Keeping a secret for a child and being a caring adult is not an option in many cases. There were instances when kids shared stories of abuse they had encountered. They wanted someone to confide in, but as a caring adult, it is my responsibility to ensure that no further risk or damage is done to them. This meant breaking that student's trust. Many times that did not feel good to me.

I had many traumatic experiences as a young person, so those moments took me back to the roots of my own central traumas. Despite personal feelings, it was not my place to judge what happened next in those students' lives, though I believed the path forward could be tumultuous. I had a major change in my life when my brother shared with our 7th-grade teacher the abuse I experienced at home. Yes, I went to foster care. Yes, it was challenging. Yes, I am okay. And yes, I was safer in foster care than where I was.

Even more so, believing that you know better for a student than their parents is a mistake and does not protect a child. At times, the secret that a student has shared with us has an implication for their parents, and we are uncomfortable sharing with them what was said. First, employ your school counselor who has more training in these types of situations. Second, don't assume that you know a parent's response. You can be respectful of the relationship that you have with the student by giving them a heads up before sharing what they've told you with another adult or even their parents. However, don't decide for a parent. That is their child and they deserve the right to know what is going on with their child and to protect them. If you know that these kinds of things are uncomfortable for you, ask them not to share with you or invite a trusted colleague into the conversation. If you want to maintain the relationship and struggle with these things, it's okay to ask them not to share with you.

Often, when kids disclose things to us, it stabs us in the heart. Our hearts for kids are strong, and we care for kids deeply in terms of meaningful thought. We also tend to cast our own trauma onto kids and feel a need to protect the younger version of ourselves. Stand firm in knowing that your presence in a child's life to intervene is valuable and validating their words and experiences is a good thing. Having an adult they can trust enough to share their experiences is valuable. It is what you are required to do. Continue to be an affirming adult for children.

To be clear, I am referring to secrets regarding things that comprise a student's well-being and safety. If a student expresses something to you that is developmentally appropriate, you don't need to call their parents. But if a student tells you that Aunt Sally thinks she is their girlfriend, that is a red flag. It is not the same as a kid telling you that Marc from Newspaper class is their boyfriend.

I've seen instances where students shared something in a language that the teacher didn't immediately translate, but the teacher missed the message the student was expressing. Listen closely, and ask students to clarify what they mean if you are unsure. Modern children are emotionally expressive. Use that to ask them to clarify what they're expressing so that you can clearly understand what they are trying to confide in you.

Care Tips

1. Consult your school's counselor or a school administrator before calling a parent with sensitive information.

2. When sharing with parents, tell them what is true and listen.

3. Avoid oversharing your opinion or analysis of what this means.

4. Parents often know details that we aren't privy to.

5. Don't immediately assume the worst of a parent.

Improvisational Language

1. Thank you for telling me this. The most important thing is that you are safe and cared for. I need to share this with someone else.

2. Is there anyone you are worried about knowing that you told me this?

3. Did you share this with anyone else?

4. Who else do you feel comfortable knowing this?

Improvisational Language for Parents

Hi, my name is Mrs. Preyan. I'm Lou's teacher. I need to share something with you that Lou told me today. What I need to share with you is a sensitive subject. May I continue?

CONNECT WITH PARENTS

*G*oing back to Robert's funeral, I remember looking over at his mother as she wept as any mother would do. I had to face a reality that no matter how much pain I was experiencing, it was barely fractional in comparison to her reality. At times, our familial energy will prompt a student to call us mom or dad.

However, parents are indescribably valuable in a child's life. They are the most important stakeholders. Over the years, I've been guilty of incorrectly assigning less than fair words and thoughts to parents as they supported their children through the transitions of life. We take on the task of caring for children in the school building every day, but we do not replace their parents.

In moments of frustration, we often criticize parents who are doing the absolute best job they can to care for their child while caring for themselves, other family members, trying to explore their own interests, and meeting their own basic needs. Shaming parents as they navigate the same rocky times that we are navigating does not operate from the same place of kindness or understanding that we're asking for. We have the privilege of joining a parent's village on their journey with their child and we should hold that space graciously.

Today, there is a wider variance in how parents raise their children. I've seen jokes and memes online describing how a parent's child would have never made it in their generation. Many parents are rethinking their approach to raising their children in favor of gentle and collaborative parenting as opposed to authoritarian parenting. It's nearly impossible to know how a parent is raising their child without speaking to them.

When I encounter children who have challenges, my first call to parents is to ask them how their child has experienced school thus far—what works and what doesn't work. Parents deserve the right to know your experiences working with their child, whether academic or social, as they have watched the progression of their child's development.

As middle school educators, we would often experience children at the onset of puberty and change. An eleven-year-old and a fourteen-year-old are developmentally years apart. I'd often explain to parents that their pre-teen was developing new interests due to the social world they were encountering. When a parent would say "my child would never do this," I'd express that your eight-year-old would not, but your twelve-year-old absolutely would.

There is a ton of mistrust today amongst parents and schools. Schools represent the old regime and ways of thinking to many parents. Many parents have their own school-based trauma that laces the interactions you are having with them. As mentioned before, if we're unable to strengthen the relationship between parents and schools, there will be more families seeking alternative schooling methods. It's true that public education is at risk. Parents are more protective of the voices that they want their children to be influenced by. I'm not saying whether that's a good or bad thing, but I want to acknowledge it.

Even more so, the acronym CARE relates to modern parents also. They, too, seek choice, access, and relationship. We know just how emotionally expressive parents can be. Remember that they raised your modern students and gave them these values. Some parents use loaded language that can feel demeaning and leave us feeling unappreciated. Much of their response is related to them not feeling cared for as a parent. Parents who have access to information about their students tend to draw less negative conclusions. Entering into meaningful relationships with students and their parents makes a ton of difference in difficult moments with students.

How does connecting with parents demonstrate care?

For a long time in urban education, we were seeking for parents to be more involved. With the COVID pandemic, we were meeting parents that we never had before. Rightfully so; many of us were nervous about the long-term effects of the pandemic. We feared that parents would be trying to tell us how to do our job as opposed to helping us control their kids (I'm sure you can see the issue with that thinking). Temporarily, this felt uncomfortable.

However, parents can't fix what they don't know. As we seek to eliminate further harm to students, we have to position ourselves as partners. We are temporary characters in a child's life. Our job is to hold the line steady for parents and to move them forward academically towards the goals they share with their larger support system.

We are more likely to call parents to report behavioral challenges than academic challenges. There are lots of reasons for that. Only one of those reasons is that the behavioral challenges trigger us. Parents deserve to know the onset of deficiencies in their students' lives, whether they be academic or social. You have the option of keeping in touch with students, but it is not a requirement of even being a caring adult. Many parents would love to make interventions in their students' academic lives but have no idea that the challenges exist.

Your input is valuable. You've worked with hundreds of ten-year-olds. A parent may only have one ten-year-old. You can help parents understand what is abnormal for their child's age and how they compare to their contemporaries. The combination of your experience with students and their experience with their child is a needed lens.

I know some parents have challenges providing care to their children. I'm a product of the foster care system myself. I know how important it is to help parents find the wraparound services that they need through your school's counselor, faith-based groups, and neighborhood initiatives. Your role is to care as best as you can. Again, join the village with grace.

Care Tips

1.   While you may be an expert on middle schoolers, parents are experts on their children.

2.   Parenting doesn't come with a manual. The nuances of child development are complex. As you develop relationships with students' parents, help them through understanding that.

3. Parents need to hear that you know their child. Use accurate adjectives and avoid loaded language.

4. Avoid calling a parent when you are angry, triggered, or not in a position for conversation.

5. Based on the age group you teach, you may spend time with hundreds of 10 years old at a time. A parent may have only encountered one 10-year-old in their life. Be kind and understanding when you offer advice to parents. How would they possibly know better?

6. After you and a student agree on what has occurred, let kids communicate with their parents what they have done. If you all see the event differently, the student will say that you are lying on them.

7. When a student tells their parents you're lying on them, what they really mean is that this doesn't feel like an accurate depiction of my intentions.

Improvisational Language

1. What do you want to be true for your child?

2. Can you tell me about some things that you've tried at home that have worked?

3. Can you tell me about some things that past teachers have done that worked?

4. Who does your child look up to?

5. I love that Lou is passionate. I'd like to share with you how his passion for cars showed up today in class.

6. Lou and I just discussed something that occurred today in class, I'll allow him to share this with you.

SEE THE WHOLE CHILD

*K*ids are complex and they are never one thing. During my time as an administrator, I worked with a young man who often needed to be restrained by adults. When he felt that he was in danger, he would kick, flail his arms, knock things over, scream, and curse. He was uncoordinated and found humor in inappropriate sayings for shock value. He loved the use of Chromebooks because they provided access to the larger world. At times, he could use the internet to explore all of his interests, no matter how inappropriate they were. He was technologically savvy and found his way around firewalls and district security measures. We often assign one adjective to kids, but that adjective doesn't allow us to see that child as a dynamic character. Okay, a quick reading lesson.

Dynamic characters undergo a significant change in literature. Think of the ways that Ebeneezer Scrooge or Shrek change in their respective stories. Dynamic characters typically change as the result of a significant event. In contrast, static characters remain the same throughout the bodies of work. Think of the bad guy from any Marvel series or Squidward from "Spongebob."

Round characters are multilayered. Think of any leading character in a sitcom such as Rachel from "Friends." We see round sitcom characters in different environments and the writer portrays them with various traits from early on. In contrast, flat characters only have a few traits—think of Joey and Phoebe also from "Friends." They have a leading trait of goofiness that is viewed first with very few deviations from this central arch. They're often comedic characters who make the same sort of jokes over and over again—think Cole from "Martin" or Kramer from "Seinfield."

One of the most entertaining things about '90s sitcoms is the moment in which one of the flat characters is suddenly assigned a new character trait that is in direct contrast to how we view them. Suddenly, Kramer is calm, collected, wise, and sensible. Marlon hits his head and is now sharing geography fun facts or Jerry Seinfield suddenly isn't funny anymore. Or the episode of "Spongebob" when Patrick dislodges his head and mistakenly attaches brain coral and is suddenly a genius. The caveat here is that kids are not characters. In schools, we tend to assign students as static or dynamic, round or flat.

We incorrectly see kids as one specific trait, leaving us incapable of viewing them as anything besides the most negative traits that they exhibit. Again, caring educators understand that kids are complex and never one thing. Liam was also lonely. He deeply wanted to have a friend. Later in my career, when I encountered a student similar to Liam who had a close friend who understood and affirmed his quirkiness, my heart ached for Liam even more. I saw the difference having just one friend made. One time when Liam had come back from suspension, I noticed he was trying to restrain himself from hugging me even though his suspension was for kicking me in the stomach.

In schools, we tend to place kids into these categories. There are a few main characters in each grade level who are dynamic. We see them undergo dynamic changes in their matriculation through school. There are a few round characters who captivate us from the moment they step into our school building. These kids are usually highly personable and we see their layers because they are boisterous and take up space in each room that they enter.

We tend to see kids like Liam as flat and static. We see them as one singular trait and have a hard time seeing them as anything else. Because this generation is relational, they can feel that. Kids deserve to be dynamic, flat, round, and static. They're not characters, they're humans. When I accepted that

Liam really needed a friend, I approached him differently not expecting the same behaviors that I'd seen many times before.

Even when he was in my office for disciplinary purposes, I asked him about his day, family, and made conversation about Roblox. He didn't need to be punished with loneliness because he was already lonely. He did need to understand that his feeling of loneliness was driving his behavior and that he needed ways to approach kids for more appropriate friendships. I fear what kind of individuals are lurking on the other side of the computer screen that he clings to. If he needed a friend just for a moment to talk about Roblox, I was okay with doing that. It also didn't mean that he wouldn't receive whatever consequence was deemed necessary for his actions.

How Does Seeing the Whole Child Demonstrate Care?

When we fail to see the whole child, we have less interest in them. Meaningful interest in a child increases our empathy towards them. We have more patience with them. We're more willing to allow them to enter our spaces to explore their interests. I've seen many instances when we fail to listen or hear the perspective of a specifically labeled student in favor of another student's side of the story.

I saw this same phenomenon with Marian. Similar to Liam, Marian was largely uncoordinated. She was a hallway runner for what I believed was no reason. When she went to the restroom, she ran. She was not in a rush, she just did it. She was always moving quickly. Once when she was feeling particularly uncoordinated and unfocused, I took her to see the newly hatched chickens in our school. She burst into the room in her typical fashion, and when I asked the teacher to hand her the very small delicate chick, I was nervous. I feared that she would be too rough.

Suddenly, when the teacher transferred the chick into her hands, it seemed like the world slowed down. Marian used only the tip of her index figure to lightly stroke the top of the chick's feather-covered head. She was still, she was quiet. I had never seen her in that way. After that moment, I noticed more and more that she was often moving slowly and hiding in the background, and then suddenly running. I just simply never noticed because I was always looking for the character I assigned to her in my own psyche.

When I started to look closer, I saw signs of autism. Helping her mother navigate the classification set off a lightbulb, and the revelation that Marian could have been on the autism spectrum helped her entire family. We have to know the kids that are in our care. When we sum them up in a few words like "that kid is bad," we fail to open our eyes up to other nuances of the child. If we took a more holistic approach to working with kids, we would have a great aid to families as we use our expertise to support them in understanding their own children. It changed the trajectory of Marian's life.

Each of our students deserves to be seen singularly and holistically as dynamic and round and, on some tough days, static and flat. It drains us emotionally when we have "that kid" in our first-period course and can't seem to see him without the label that our mind innocently places on him.

Care Tips

1. Use accurate adjectives to describe kids.

2. Use accurate words to describe kids' behaviors, especially when you speak to parents.

3. Ask a trusted colleague who has a positive relationship with the student if you are missing something or have any blind spots.

4. Acknowledge when you have a contentious relationship with a specific student and work with them in private or after taking a few deep breaths.

Improvisational Language

1. Hey, I notice that you're _____ today, but yesterday you were _____. Am I missing something?

2. How would you describe yourself today?

3. Even though you are _____, I need you to be _____. How can I help you with that?

OPERATE GENUINELY

*D*uring my first year as a school administrator, I was unsure of who I was supposed to be. This was nearing the end of traditional discipline having an effect on kids and still resonating with parents. I was 27 years old and working through my own feelings of imposter syndrome. I am certain I was wearing my infamous black blazer and pencil skirt suit.

This time though, I was wearing a pair of black sketchers that are designed for the comfort of walking in my new administrator life. My apple watch was nestled under my blazer so I could be reached by whoever needed me, my radio was on the right channel, and I was ready to prove that I belonged in that corner office on the third floor of the building. Eventually, the moment that I was anticipating came. A teacher sent two kids to me that were disrupting class, and I prepared to put on the show.

When you are working through challenging situations as a novice practitioner, you are lacking language. You don't know what to say or what to do. You know that you're supposed to be the one solving the problem, you just don't know how yet. I channeled a former administrator who I had admired from my earlier days in education and figured that was who I was supposed to be. His approach always worked and teachers seemed to trust that he would "handle" kids.

When Joseph and Yadira arrived in my office, I emulated speeches that I heard stern administrators give. "I'm not going to take all this foolishness. You can be at the house for the next three days." And then, I did something I'm sure I have only seen in a movie somewhere, but I was deep into character and I had to see it through. I swept my arms across my desk, knocking everything onto the floor. "I'm not having it!" I yelled. The two students looked at each other, nearly smirking and nearly buying it. I continued my no-nonsense speech and then sent them back to class.

Here is a fun fact: if you sweep all of the items on your desk to the ground in an attempt to appear like you're in charge, you have to pick all of those items up. I spent a lot of time perfectly arranging the items on my desk to ensure that I would appear as a person of power. I caddy cornered the post-it notes so I could quickly take notes from my important phone calls. There was a school mug with pens so I could underline things twice, which is the ultimate symbol of seriousness. After my show of fragile power, I picked up my nameplate, office phone that was still dangling by the cord, various colored post-it notes, leftover "Meet the Teacher Night" sign-in sheets, and all of the trinkets that I placed on my desk to make it appear that I was powerful—yet artistic enough—to have trinkets on my desk. I never felt weaker than at that moment. To top it off, the continuous accordion-style design of post notes made it harder and harder for me to pick them up.

I kept some of this facade up for all of two weeks. In the cafeteria, I would watch intensely, scowl, and stare students in the eyes to maintain a sense of mysteriousness to them. I mean besides, if teachers can't smile until Christmas, administrators can't smile until Valentine's Day. This was my absolute worst moment as a school administrator, solely because I wasn't being myself. Today's relational kids don't go for that. I have seen teachers and administrators from all walks of life, skin tones, and personalities command a room of children and lead adults. Kids respond to people who are operating in who they genuinely are and they have a special ability to call out malarkey when they see it.

I've seen many teachers try to channel another type of disciplinarian when they encounter a difficult moment with a student. What I didn't realize is that the individual I was channeling was being authentic to who they were, and I would need to do the same. I have been in awe of many colleagues I have worked with during my tenure in education, and often I'd say to myself, "If I can be like so-and-so then I'd do it right." As a caring educator, you don't need to be like anyone else; you only need to be yourself.

Since that day, I have had many students sent to my office, and my approach has since changed. Now, I lead with questions. "What do I need to know? Am I missing something?" I don't scream or yell (that often). I listen first because that's who I am as a human being. I don't seek to represent myself as overly tough or stern; I only seek to present myself as a loving, caring adult who will have to redirect you and discipline you if you have done something wrong. That has taken me further than any other approach because I don't have to rehearse it. I just have to be. Pretending is exhausting.

There is, undoubtedly, a place to learn from the individuals around us who we respect. Again, attempting to perform as someone else is exhausting. Believing that who you are is not enough is draining. At your core, as a loving educator, kids will understand you. Even if they've never met a human like you in the entire world, they have now. I have seen many educators envy the energetic, personable educator who students love to line up outside their door to do their special handshake. That doesn't have to be you if that's not who you are. If you are calm, awkward, soft-spoken, strange, loud, monotone, whatever... be that. And be it good.

I debated telling this story, and I only tell it because if you're still reading, I have confidence that you are truly a caring educator and you understand the wide range of nuances that have contributed to urban communities. I ask that you only read this story with understanding and empathy.

"Ms. Preyan, did your baby daddy pay for your nails?"

"No, sweetheart, I'm married. My husband paid for them."

"Ms. Preyan, that's why I like you. You're different."

I was stuck in my tracks for a moment. I was taken aback that Laniyah considered me different because I was married. There were many times when I wasn't certain that I was reaching this student, and I was even more confused that this was the moment that she made a positive expression to me, and it was in no way related to what I had been trying to preach to her all year long. I understood that day that my genuine presence alone was a service to students.

Kids need to see a variety of people. What we should understand is that many kids live in communities that are near monoliths. Meaning, regardless of their background of either racial or class groups, their community is likely full of people who share their way of thinking and life. The only Pacific Islander that they have ever met who loves hydrangeas, is a nerdy athlete, and Muslim may be in a school setting. Years later, when they encounter another individual like you, they'll have a genuine positive point of reference to pull from. They'll understand more about the diverse world of people and even the diversity among people of the same races, genders, and backgrounds. As caring educators of modern kids, we give kids safe access to the larger world, and we should do so as genuinely as we can.

How Does Operating Genuinely Demonstrate Care?

Part of our challenge today is believing that we need the old-school educators back. Those educators operated in response to the needs of their time. They served the community in the ways that the community asked to be served. Schools are the funnel for young people into society. Back then, those teachers often had the support of many parents in their approach because that authoritarian style resonated with the times. Most of us are not our parents or grandparents and we see the world differently because our world is different. Education as a public service raises students to enter the world of today, not yesterday. Our commitment to authenticity as a society has to mimic what we do in the school system.

Showing meaningful interest in kids begins with showing meaningful interest in yourself. When we show up as our true selves, we allow students to see safe expressions of individuality. When we take care of ourselves, we do a better job taking care of the kids. When I was a young teacher struggling to find my voice, a seasoned colleague gave me great advice. There is Shirley and there is Ms. Bolden, and the best version of you is Shirley Bolden.

Caring for kids does fatigue us. Trying to behave like someone else only adds to the exhaustion. There is space for you as a professional teacher to be yourself. I've seen teachers who loved jiu-jitsu, anime, origami, spiders, planes, memes, yoga, rugby, fish tanks, improv comedy, and Marvel make connections with kids by bringing their whole selves into their work.

CALL YOUR OWN BIAS

*I*t's our job as educators to care for every student in our building. But, I have to admit that some students were a bit harder to connect with. Some kids came from subpopulation groups in our society, and I didn't have much experience interacting with those groups. I perceived that we had different political beliefs and moral systems. Some families operated in norms that I believed were harmful and reminded me of past pains. Some of their parents weaponized their words in ways that I didn't agree with.

As human beings, we all have some sort of bias and preference. We all have beliefs and preferences that are not limited to time management, language, dress, and our personal space. When I would present school discipline practices at yearly professional development, I would often start with asking educators to identify their triggers related to these items. This is important because our triggers are connected to our biases.

My personal biases relate to the tone and language that kids use with adults. Some kids have ways of expression that I was raised to see as incorrect or less than. Because I lived with my grandmother from ages six to twelve, I have traditional beliefs about language expression with adults. My grandmother would tell us that she would "wash our mouths out with soap" if we spoke in a certain tone. Later when I worked with certain students, I had to check my biases to ensure that I wasn't failing to care for those students.

I can remember working with a teacher who was always incredibly polished and neat. She valued physical experience and made sure that every student tucked their shirts in perfectly when they entered her classroom. She was unapologetic in that. Eventually, she recognized that the practice was getting in the way of her relationships with students, and many of their parents often greeted her with expressive language to express their disdain for the policy. When she noticed that it was getting in the way of her relationship with her students and parents, she began to relax her practice to remove some of the tension her bias created with some of her most difficult students. She decided that teaching her students was more important than the tension that her stringent rules were causing.

How Does Calling Your Own Bias Demonstrate Care?

Our biases should not change the way we provide care to kids. We are more prone to provide meaningful care to kids to whom we feel the most connected. When I met Jasmine, I knew that she and I would bump heads. Jasmine was the embodiment of emotional expressiveness. She was organized, social, funny, perceptive, and direct. She was outwardly expressive in a way that I was never able to be as a child. The way that she spoke to adults in positions of power was uncommon to me. She would speak over me, yell, and sometimes curse.

Once when I interacted with her and her father, I said, "Jasmine, do not speak to me that way."

"No!" her father yelled, "You need to let her speak her mind."

I was in shock. Her father corrected me and insisted that I needed to listen to her as she gave me a piece of her twelve-year-old mind. Without question, I had to swallow my pride and preferences. Double ouch.

When I interacted with Jasmine, I would often have to pause and think meaningfully about how I responded to her. She was also a fast talker, and when I spoke slowly, she spoke louder. I was not able to remove the way I cared for her because I didn't enjoy the way that she spoke. I had to recognize the bias that I carried. On Jasmine's last day, we had the most meaningful connection. I let her know that her voice was strong and that I wanted her to use it in a way that would be productive to our entire society. Her voice did not need to be silenced. As a caring educator, I had to realize that it needed to be curated.

Care Tips

1. Be honest with yourself about your biases and triggers.
2. Pay attention to your responses to subgroups of kids.
3. Check in with a trusted colleague to monitor your blind spots.

Improvisational Language

1. Hey Ms. Johnson, Lou is in my third-period class and we don't have the best relationship. Is there something that I'm missing?
2. Ms. Johnson, when I am working with Lou, he tends to get under my skin. If you see us interacting, can you watch and give me some feedback?
3. Can you help me with Lou? I'm not certain I can be fair to him today.

CORRECT OTHERS AND EMPATHIZE WITH THOSE AROUND YOU

Kids are many things. They can be caring, goofy, clumsy, curious, anxious, shy, adventurous, and thrill seekers. Because kids have to survive the world they were born into, without fault, they can also be stubborn, mistrusting, careless, selfish, aloof, and combative. I can give you thousands of adjectives to describe kids. There is one that I will not use, "bad." During my early years in education, there was a teacher at the end of the hall from me. She made strong statements about kids. "That little boy is bad." Then she made a statement that still stings my ears, "That kid is going to end up dead or in jail."

At the very basic level, kids are always innocent. There is a strange reality in our society that has always bothered me. Children are born into a certain set of circumstances and they develop based on those circumstances. Kids who are stealing food because they are hungry are not criminals, they should have never been left hungry. Kids who have been silenced are bound to yell at someone at some point. On the contrary, kids have to learn how to exist in the world with the support of caring adults. Once a child turns eighteen years old, all of the realities of how adults have contributed to them become their fault. This is why it's incredibly important to teach kids how to operate in a world with all of their adjectives—positive and negative.

Most of the negative behaviors that students engage in are the result of their negative experiences. Behavior is communication. To survive those negative feelings and experiences they've encountered, they tend to work with the resources they have, like their voices. As a child, they're not exactly able to unpack all of that. As caring adults, we know enough about our own experiences and the root causes of some of *our* behaviors to have empathy for them.

How Does Correcting Others Demonstrate Care?

As caring educators, we are called to lessen the risk and damage to kids as we care for them. It's why we have to correct others. We correct and support other adults when they carelessly assign adjectives to kids without consideration of the root cause. We correct and support parents when they are trying to make sense of the new patterns that they see in their children.

I never corrected the teacher at the end of the hall when she called kids "bad." I had a huge heart for kids but didn't think I had the right to correct her. I hated that I heard her voice at Robert's funeral. Despite my hesitation, reducing harm means correcting others. When we fail to correct others, we allow kids to be in spaces with people who have biases and prejudice against them. Kids learn from everyone around them. Those negative thoughts that we have about kids permeate every interaction that we have with them. When kids ask to go to the restroom, their motives are questioned. When they ask for water, they are questioned, and it contributes to the Matthew Effect.

Let me be piercingly clear: I am not saying that kids are without fault. Kids are kids, and they will find ways to do things they prefer to do like meeting a friend in the bathroom or throwing a piece of paper across the room. As educators, we are still required to do the basics of supervision which is a component of care. Along the path, we have to partner with other educators who are also making sense of their own paths.

When we allow others around us to label kids, it slowly eats away at our psyche. We start to believe the things that those teachers say about those kids. Remember: kids can be dynamic and round, not just flat and static. Many kids are searching for someone in the building who allows them to feel cared for. Just as we correct kids who say mean things about students, we should do the same when adults do it.

Even more so, many of us are still transitioning from the old ways of operating with kids. We're all deconstructing old beliefs and systems that no longer serve us. Many of our own language patterns were formed in our childhoods. We know how adults spoke to us. We remember very vividly those who used their words to uplift us and those who used their words to tear us down. It's important for us to empathize with those around us as they unpack that.

As a school administrator, you're tasked with resolving lots of problems that arise. Many of those problems are related to behavioral challenges. Some teachers call on administrators more than others to support them with students. As an administrator, there is something we all have to hear. Working with a student one-on-one in your office without all of the stimulants of the classroom is different from working with a student in the classroom. This is true of working with kids in a physical education class, math class, chemistry class, or robotics.

A tough lesson for me was to empathize with others around me. When we see others struggling through the new existing dynamics in education, refrain from passing judgment. Accept that it may take them a bit longer to deconstruct the beliefs that have governed their lives for long periods of time. Join the village. Correct others when they are wrong, and lend your learning as you listen.

I challenge everyone to correct others when they use language that has negative connotations toward kids. Children can be combative, energetic, unfocused, stubborn, unorganized, silly, and nonchalant. None of those things disqualify them from being cared for.

When we reduce kids to negative adjectives, it decreases our meaningful interest in them. It then begins to influence how we teach that student. Imagine the gaps that can be created in a child's life if their elementary reading and math teachers hold negative views about them and no one calls them in.

Care Tips

1. Call colleagues in, not out.

2. Call parents in, not out.

3. Ask the teacher or parent if it's a good time to talk.

4. Consider the receiver before sending emails and text messages.

Improvisational Language

1. I heard you describe Lou as a rotten kid. Could you rephrase that?

2. It seems like you're venting right now, would you like for me to just listen right now?

EXPECT PROGRESS, NOT PERFECTION

*M*any new and valuable strategies are helping us with the new school rules. Nearly all of the new strategies, restorative justice, circles, and discretionary discipline are good. They promote the choice, relationship and emotional expression that these students are accustomed to. Most of these strategies are rooted in dismantling the hierarchy that has created some negative stereotypes in school with power and control. Schools often abandon strong practices because they don't work immediately. Teacher buy-in can die quickly when something doesn't work immediately. We should expect progress, but not perfection.

Michelle and Kimberly had a social media conflict that deeply and reasonably upset Kimberly. I knew that a circle was the right step to repair the relationship. The two students were beginning to create a larger issue in the grade level as kids begin to take sides as they naturally do. When I offered both students a circle, Kimberly refused.

Now, this was a true moment of learning for me. Typically, students agreed to the circle, and I've always had enough of a relationship with students to coax them if they were unsure. This was the first time I had a student refuse to be a part of a circle.

"If you put me in a room with her I'm not going to be able to control myself. I'm going to beat her up."

I believed her, and she was giving me an honest expression. I had to respect that. I understood that circles are a good thing and yield strong results. I also knew the other kids in the grade level would use this conflict for entertainment and excitement, and I needed to diffuse the grade level. Michelle was more willing. I asked her to write down her responses to the circle questions and anything that she wanted to say to Kimberly. Frankly, I was desperate and I didn't want to lose steam with her and risk reigniting the conflict.

When I went back to Kimberly, who I had a positive relationship with, I explained to her that I only needed her to listen to Michelle's apology and I wouldn't require her to say anything. Using the techniques of the circle, I allowed Kimberly to stand by the door so that she could leave if needed because she was the offended party. I started with green light-hearted questions and knew that Kimberly wouldn't answer them. I tried to stay as close to the practice as I possibly could.

Michelle read her response and Kimberly only made eye-contact with her. That was her only acknowledgment of Michelle in the room. At the end, I asked them to agree to not fight. Michelle agreed and Kimberly shook her head yes at me. The moment was far from perfect, but there was progress. As someone who was responsible for caring for both girls, I am responsible for ensuring that further damage or risk isn't done. Ensuring there wasn't another fight and allowing them to move forward to focus on academics is caring for them.

As an administrator, I am also responsible for using strategies that work for our campus and not abandoning the ship when there is limited success. A few weeks later, we had a circle for another student who had a negative relationship with an administrative staff member. When the administrator asked me to facilitate a circle with the student, my mind went back to the last failure. What if I can't get her in the room? What if my previous failures lower my confidence in the moment? Lots of uneasy thoughts rushed into my head. The student agreed but told me, "I'm not going to say much to her."

Frankly, she did exactly what she said she would do. She spoke mostly to me as the facilitator, and that was still progress. She did agree to disengage with the defiant behavior towards the administrator with the most minimal amount of eye contact that could be considered eye contact. However, the progress had to be acknowledged with the student and the practice. About three weeks later, while I was sitting with the administrator in the cafeteria, she came over and started chatting with us. We discreetly looked at each other, both understanding the significance of the moment. Progress is good and should not be belittled.

Both kids and adults have to accept that progress as a sign of good things to come. Over time, circles became more prevalent on our campus and we looked to them more often for complicated scenarios. We are always working towards progress with kids. Progress is one of the many rewards for care.

How Does Expecting Progress Demonstrate Care?

Relationships are built; that's true of all forms of relationships. In previous generations, respecting adults meant doing what they said, whenever they said it. I remember when someone suggested that kids needed respect, too, and how much debate that created in the professional development session I was attending in the late 2010s.

Relationships work when there is mutual respect. The idea of kids getting in line is long gone. Even more so, we can't get the kids in line because we no longer believe in falling in line. Instead, we should be seeking to bring the kids into relationships, cultural systems, and harmony. This is no different than what we're asking for as adults. Many of the kids will willingly join those structures. For the additional remaining five percent, we are seeking to bring them into the fold by first caring for them, and then expecting progress along the way.

Care Tips

1. Using consistent best practices and checking up on your implementation is more important than finding a new strategy.

2. New strategies are often tried and true by practitioners before they become popularized.

3. Notice progress out loud.

Improvisational Language

1. Today, I noticed that you were able to _____. That's not everything I asked for, but it is a start. Next time, we'll see if we can continue that and also_____.

2.   What part of this are you able to do today?

3.   What do you need right now to get started?

VALUE OTHER SKILLS

*L*ayla never wanted to be in class. She would find a reason to go to the restroom and would remain in the restroom until the bell rang. She was quietly recalcitrant and was not outwardly defiant. She would quietly walk away from you and make it clear that she had no intention of listening to you. She was so non-combative, you almost didn't know what to do. You just sort of stood there in disbelief because her brand of insubordination was not loud or forceful.

On the weekends, she worked with her mother at a small business delivering wedding decor. I learned this when Layla's mother came to the school in shambles because she had run away. Her mother was quiet like Layla and cried on my shoulder. I stood there unsure what to say, I had only spoken to her twice in about three years, but she knew I cared for her daughter. Layla had an undeniable leadership skill. When I gave her a complex task, she went into project management mode.

"So you want me to log on to Canva, make a ticket, email it to you so you can see it."

"Yes."

"When I finish, do I need to print and cut them?"

"Yes."

"Okay, I need at least three other people to help me cut them. But you pick the kids so I don't get distracted talking to them."

After seeing the way she worked on the ticket for the basketball game, around Halloween, I needed someone to organize the candy I planned to have delivered to all the teachers to provide for the students. Layla asked if she could do it. When I returned, Layla had created an assembly line amongst students—each of them were working quietly and she walked around making sure they were correctly mixing chocolate and fruity candy in proper proportions.

"Ms. Preyan, do you need me to go in the class with the sub to make sure they do it right?"

Now, let's be clear. Layla was a skipper. Despite this fact, she also possessed additional skills. Caring for her meant learning to celebrate those skills and leverage them to get her to stop skipping. Skipping is harmful to her success. Her teachers needed to know that she was an organizer so they could find a way to allow her to operate in that gift while in class. At times, when she came to me after skipping multiple classes, I wouldn't allow her to help. Instead, I would share an upcoming task with her so that she could redeem herself. Her skipping could not be ignored—neither could her leadership skills. It was important for me to over-communicate my disapproval of her skipping while simultaneously over-communicating my fondness of her skill set. The goal was for one door to lead to the next.

Care Tips

1. Don't ignore negative behavior in a student.

2. Describe a student's behavior with accurate, concise language.

3. Have the student repeat the accurate, concise language to you.

4. Communicate with parents in the same accurate, concise language that you use with the student.

Improvisational Language

1. Maya, I know that you _____ and I appreciate that, but you also _____ and we need to work on that.

2.   Is there anyone else that you want to know that you are good at _____.

3.   How did you get so good at _____?

4.   Is there a reason that you do _____ also?

5.   Let me help you coach you on this behavior.

CONCLUSION

$\mathcal{B}$y now, you may be tired of hearing about my failures in education. Know that I tell these stories from a place of support for you on your journey. My deepest hope is for students, parents, and administrators alike to feel cared for—for the sake of the children.

Burnout is real. I want to encourage practitioners to focus on your locus of control. We aren't able to dictate how a parent chooses to raise their child. We aren't immediately able to influence the transition of our society into a more emotionally driven world. Don't allow yourself to get stuck into the frustration of things that we can not change. Accept that some of the internal conflicts we feel in education are related to how deeply we care about kids. We feel conflicted because sometimes we do not know how to work with large groups of kids with such varying presentations. We would feel less fatigue if we had more skills.

One of the big misconceptions about our journey is that kids get away with things. Trust me, I've had moments when I strongly disagreed with the code of conduct on a student's behavior. I've had to swallow my pride when I hinted at a lengthy punishment for a student and the new updated code of conduct suggested a verbal correction. I have come to understand that much of how we think about discipline and governance in today's society is to teach kids about the root cause of their actions. The goal is to eliminate the repetition of poor behavior. Lessons have a much longer-lasting effect than an evening detention.

I know that it doesn't feel good when kids walk away while you're speaking, curse, yell, or stare off when we are giving our emotional and professional best. I know it doesn't feel good when parents don't back us up when we have pure intentions. Most of us are giving our best. The new way of life seems so mushy and soft. We're not therapists, and all of this talk of childhood trauma seems to be asking us to do one too many things. We're *teachers*.

In caring for yourself, every day when you head to your car, ask yourself this question: Did I do my best to care for the children? If the answer is "yes," rest easy. If you can see a gap in your practice regarding supervising, eliminating the possibility or risk of harm, and your meaningful interest in children, try again to give your best the next day to provide more delicate care. Remind yourself that the children of this generation are driven by choice, access, relationship, and emotions. We chose that reality for them because we saw the gap in our society. This transition is uncomfortable, but it is necessary.

I'll end this with this. Teachers and administrators, if no one is telling you this, I will. Teachers are valuable members of our society. Teaching is a sacred career that is deserving of the highest reverence. Teaching is both a science and an art; it's one of the most layered jobs in the world. Teachers and school leaders have some of the most diverse skill sets of all professionals. Schools have some of the longest-lasting effects on us as human beings. The kids need you. They need great schools filled with great people. The parents need you and our larger society needs you. If no one else is saying it, thank you. And don't worry, we're all going to be okay.

CPSIA information can be obtained
at www.ICGtesting.com
Printed in the USA
BVHW031515131022
649370BV00013B/1043

9 798218 066703